Well Done!

by

Dr. Leon van Rooyen

© Dr. Leon van Rooyen 2011

All rights reserved. No part of this book may be reproduced, stored in a retrieval system, or transmitted in any form or by any means-electronic, mechanical, photocopying, recording, or otherwise-without prior permission in writing from the copyright holder except as provided by USA copyright law.

ISBN 978-1-935298-77-9

Truth Book Publishers
824 Bills Rd
Franklin, IL 62638
877-649-9092
www.truthbookpublishers.com

1. Book - Religion   2. Education   3. Inspirational

First Printing 2011

Printed in the United States of America

DEDICATION

This book is dedicated to all my staff who have labored so diligently with me in the harvest. Many of them have been working with me for years, some in a salaried position and others as volunteers. The accomplishments of Global Ministries and Relief are due to God's grace and their efforts.

All of the staff who are presently employed and those who have previously been employed have all contributed to the work and did so as true servants of the Lord Jesus Christ. They have sacrificed, worked long hours, traveled many miles and as result thousands of leaders have been trained, churches planted, souls saved, schools established and students enrolled. This book is dedicated to each one.

Global Ministries and Relief has been a fruitful ministry, and all the glory goes to God. My thanks goes to my team who each do their part with a spirit of excellence. When the records of eternity are published for all to read, their labor, prayer and diligence will be revealed. I want to say thank you here so that when I am there, all my thanks may be directed to Him who sits at the right hand of the Father, the Lamb of God.

Well done you good and faithful servants.

I want to express my thanks to some individuals who have all contributed to this book finally being published.

I trust that my memory won't fail me, so if I did leave you out please forgive me.

Thank you to Beverly Tivin for her service to the Master and to me as my dedicated editor. The truth be told, I would not have a book published without her devotion and motivation that she gave to me during the process. Thank you to my youngest son, Matthew, for his creative work in designing the cover. Thank you to Jeff Crandall for his photographic work for the back cover. Thank you to Peter Innes, Beth Yost and Rachael Osborne in their work to turn this book into an eBook. Thank you to our publishers, Faith Publishers, for their professional service in the layout and printing. Thank you James and JaNell!

I would like to also thank renowned author and prophetic preacher, Robert Paul Lamb, for his kind introduction. I was inspired by his constructive ideas and his enthusiasm for the subject and content. He was very gracious and most kind. Finally, thank you to my friend, partner in the work, and an outstanding pastor, Elhadj Diallo for his comments.

Dr. Leon van Rooyen

TABLE OF CONTENTS

Foreword i

Endorsement iv

Introduction v

Chapter 1 - The Ministry of the Bowl and Towel 1

Chapter 2 - Serving from the Position of Wholeness .. 21

Chapter 3 – Not all who Serve are Servants 41

Chapter 4 - The Attitude of a Servant 61

Chapter 5 - The Anointing of a Servant 89

Chapter 6 - The Motive of a Servant 107

Chapter 7 - Promotion and Commendation 123

Chapter 8 - Becoming More Like Jesus 137

FOREWORD

Dr. Leon van Rooyen has "unearthed" an aspect of the life and ministry of Jesus in his book, *Well Done!* that is seldom taught in the modern Church. He wisely labels that ministry "the bowl and towel," correctly identifying the servant-hearted life of our Savior. *Well Done!* is a broad-reaching study, rich in personal anecdotes and resplendent in its scope of presenting the Word of God on the life-changing subject of servanthood.

With the insight and experience of a skilled surgeon, Dr. Leon dissects the trouble with many believers who serve unhappily in a local church until they are offended and explode. He concludes, "What in the past was pleasant will soon become an offense." Every pastor will agree with the correctness of that statement. In fact, as I read this material, I secretly wished that I had been exposed to this kind of revelation in the days when I was engaged in pastoral ministry. These truths will be invaluable to every believer, but particularly helpful to five-fold ministers, especially pastors. This book describes the secret to the Apostle Paul's magnificent ministry—*"I have made myself a servant to all"* (1 Corinthians 9:19). Dr. Leon wisely connects the dots to Jesus in quoting Paul's words—*"Let this mind be in you which was also in Christ Jesus"* (Philippians 2:5).

As the author of multiple books on the lives of some of God's most visible ministers, I found myself in agreement with Dr. Leon's comments: "Some pastors and church leaders are far removed from the people, as if the people existed for the leaders rather than the other way around."

At the heart of his study is his definition of ministry. It is serving. Additionally, he expands that definition to a simple sentence: It is doing what needs to be done when it needs to be done. What a statement!

Dr. Leon accentuates the lasting value of humility, saying: "It is from a position of humility that we will most readily be received." His story about winning the world with a toilet brush in one hand and a Bible in the other is a classic. Truly, the symbol of serving in the Kingdom of God—the bowl and the towel—is a symbol of great power.

He is right on the money when he says that we have no right to lead unless we can properly serve. His examples of Joshua, Elisha and, of course, Jesus, are flawless. The way to grow and the way to promotion in God is to be a servant.

The beauty of this book is not just that it is a Christ-centered, Bible-based approach to the subject of serving. That, in itself, would be worth the price of the material. The beauty is that this book's author—Bible school director, missionary, pastor, teacher—lives by this model of serving.

Personally, I am greatly challenged by Dr. Leon's book, believe strongly that it is "a word in season" for the Body of Christ, and am particularly pleased to endorse this volume to every child of God. Applying these principles will be life-altering for those who dare to believe and live by such truths!

Robert Paul Lamb

ENDORSEMENT

I first encountered Dr. Leon in 2001 at a conference in the local church in Calgary where I was serving in evangelism, the cleaning team, and ushering. Teaching a series on servanthood, his words were simple yet profound. On the second night when he called me forward to present me with a toilet brush and a Bible, he said, "With a toilet brush and a Bible you will change the world." These words strengthened and touched something in me. I had always served with all my heart, but from that point on, I felt the Lord was acknowledging my call as a servant to Him and to the people. Something new was imparted to me.

This teaching has changed my life. I reconnected with Dr. Leon in 2007. By this time I had been leading the church for two years. Dr. Leon has been a father to us both. His love and care are so real as he helped us in consulting, teaching, guiding, advising, and establishing. He has invested generously in our lives and church with no strings attached. For me, he stands tall as a man of God who carries an anointing to raise up the new generation. The content of this book is what has brought maturity and empowerment to my life and ministry. I fully endorse it, and I know that the same anointing that impacted me and our church will empower you and take you to the next level of ministry.

Elhadj Diallo, Overseer of Crosspointe Organization and Co-pastor of Crosspointe Fellowship Church in Calgary, Canada

INTRODUCTION

Unless the Lord returns in our generation, we will all die. You may say, "Leon, what a weird way to start a book, talking about dying." In actuality though, this book is about living. It is about living your life to the full and making it count for eternity. You do not want to live your life in such a mediocre way that you just make it into heaven without any reward; rather, you want to live with such a sense of eternity in your heart that everything you do will count and will be to the glory of God. This book is filled with vital insights that can change your life **if** you allow them to.

All born-again believers will see the Lord one day. At that glorious moment our hearts will overflow with the anthem, "Worthy is the Lamb who was slain for my salvation." Once we have worshiped Him, we Christians will be judged, not for our sins, but for our rewards. What words would you like to hear Jesus say to you? Remember, we are not saved by our works but our works do count for eternity.

"Well done, good and faithful...servant."

Without a doubt, the words we long to hear are, "Well done, good and faithful servant." We have heard this expression so often that we barely even notice that it is the **servant** whom Jesus commends. When you break down these simple words, you will see that they imply the following:

- That you did something.

- That you were a servant.

- That you were a good servant.

- That you were a faithful servant.

Jesus will not say "Well done!" to everyone, but only to those who have done something and done it well. He is not obliged to commend us, if we have not done our part or have been lazy and uninvolved in the work of the Kingdom. Our society is so politically correct and yet so incorrect. This generation has been affirmed and indulged to the point that whenever anything is said that brings correction or discipline, people fall apart.

Though a serving lifestyle should be a basic, integral part of our walk with God, for many Christians it is a burdensome obligation that is easier to simply ignore. The glamour and excitement attached to such subjects as the anointing, signs and wonders, and prophecy (to name but a few) is missing from servanthood. Those subjects certainly have their place, but they must operate beneath the garment of a servant. Our message is the gospel, but our lifestyle is that of a servant.

For we do not preach ourselves, but Christ Jesus the Lord, and ourselves your bondservants for Jesus' sake. (2 Corinthians 4:5)

You might wonder why there is a need to study the importance and implications of being a servant. After all, what is there to say about it beyond the admonition that all Christians must get out there and serve? This book was not written as a pep talk so that you will go and do your "religious" duty. Instead, it was designed to bring a whole new perspective toward serving from the revelation of this powerful truth: being a servant is actually the way of the Master and the path to God's greatness! The Lord is not pleased with mere outward behavior but looks upon the heart. If you want to be just like Jesus, you will be a servant, because you have His heart, not because you want to impress Him that you have turned into a do-gooder. We can serve grudgingly, getting annoyed when we feel that we are being inconvenienced, or we can serve with joy and gladness of heart, as He Himself commands (Deuteronomy 28:47).

It is my hope that as you proceed through the chapters of this book, your conduct and attitude toward serving will undergo a transformation such that you become that servant who will one day hear those coveted words from the lips of Jesus, "Well done, good and faithful servant."

On a recent flight to minister in Bloomington, Illinois, the woman sitting next to me introduced herself as a believer and asked if I was a pastor. She was not being intrusive, but regional jets leave little room but to notice what is going on around you. It seems that while

I was working on this book, she had been enthusiastically reading my laptop screen for some time. "Servanthood is certainly a topic that needs to be taught, and I like what you are saying," she remarked. I trust that her comment will be true for you and that delving into this neglected subject will inspire you to become a servant.

You have heard the saying that the way up is down. Well, becoming a servant is not going down in life but going up. Enjoy the ride!

Dr. Leon van Rooyen

Questions:

Why is the subject of becoming a servant unpopular?

Would you rather read a book on the servant lifestyle or on the anointing? Explain.

What comes to mind when you think of a being a servant?

Who comes to mind when you think of a servant?

Do you consider yourself a servant?

> What makes someone a servant?
>
>
> Do you consider serving to be spiritual? Why or why not?

Chapter 1

The Ministry of the Bowl and Towel

For most of us who have been brought up with some knowledge of the Bible, we would immediately identify the ministry of the bowl and towel as the serving ministry of Jesus. He took up the bowl and the towel and washed the disciples' dirty feet. Through this simple act, Jesus demonstrated that true greatness is found in spontaneous acts of serving others at their point of need. However, He also made it clear that this demonstration was an example for those around the table as well as all future believers. The ministry of the bowl and towel is a responsibility that Jesus has entrusted to every Christian.

It was just before the Passover Feast. Jesus knew that the time had come for him to leave this world and go to the Father. Having loved his own who were in the world, he now showed them the full extent of his love. **The evening meal was being served,** *and the devil had already prompted Judas Iscariot, son of Simon, to betray Jesus. Jesus knew that the Father had put all things under his power, and that he had come from God and was returning to God; so he got up from the meal,* **took off his outer clothing, and wrapped a towel around his waist. After that, he poured water into a basin and began to wash his disciples' feet, drying them with the towel that was wrapped around him.** *He came to Simon Peter, who said to him, "Lord, are you going to* wash my feet?" Jesus replied, "You do not realize now what I am doing, but later you will understand." "No," said Peter, "you shall never wash my feet." Jesus answered, "Unless I wash you, you have no part with me." "Then, Lord," Simon Peter replied, "not just my feet but my hands and my head as well!" Jesus answered, "A person who has had a bath needs only to wash his feet; his whole body is clean. And you are clean, though not every one of you." For he knew who was going to betray him, and that was why he said not every one was clean. When he had finished washing their feet, he put on his clothes and returned to his place. "Do you understand what I have done for you?" he asked them. "You call me 'Teacher' and 'Lord,' and rightly so, for that is what I am. **Now that I, your Lord and Teacher, have washed your feet, you also should wash one another's feet. I have set you an example that you should do as I have done for you.** I tell you the truth, no servant is greater than his master, nor is a messenger greater than the one who sent him. Now that you know these things, you will be blessed if you do them. (John 13:1-17 NIV)

Washing feet was customary.

Why did Jesus wait until supper was already underway to wash the disciples' feet? In the Jewish culture of that day, it was unacceptable to sit at the table with dirty, smelly feet, so it was customary to have one's feet washed upon entering a house. In the above account, however, no one took the responsibility to carry out this menial chore when it should have been done. Supper was already in progress, yet their feet were still filthy.

Jesus had been a guest in the house of a Pharisee named Simon when a woman came and washed His feet with her tears, wiped them with her hair, and anointed them with oil (Luke 7:38). In response to Simon's insinuation that a prophet would not associate with a sinner such as this woman, Jesus took him to task: "When I came into your house, you didn't bathe My feet, you didn't greet me with a kiss, you didn't anoint My head." This was the expected protocol upon entering a house. In sheer abandonment of thanksgiving, this woman had accomplished what should have been done as the most basic courtesy. Those who organized the meal and the house should also have arranged for the feet of the guests to be washed. This shirking of responsibility is still characteristic of many believers today; rarely lifting a finger, they are only too happy to let someone else take care of the dirty work. Knowing the right thing and not doing it is just as unacceptable as doing the wrong thing (James 4:17).

Despite the three years of intensive training during which Jesus modeled Kingdom values and the role of a servant, His followers still failed to do what He had taught them. (Sounds like some of their relatives are still in the Church today.) Believers have no problem agreeing with some basic teachings, but they **do** have a problem when it comes to applying them. No wonder

Jesus taught that the person who applied the Word was blessed, while hearing without application was of little value (Luke 11:28).

Since Jesus would soon be going to the Cross, we can imagine what must have taken place at that Last Supper. He would review all the areas that He had taught and modeled for the disciples, because they would soon be taking charge of the future of the Church. He would give very clear instructions on the purpose of His ministry and what would lie ahead for them. He would share the outworking of the prophecies of His death and resurrection. Now He gazes into the faces of those around the table, disappointed that not even one of them did what was needed. They had followed His instructions to prepare the table and the food, but no one wanted to "stoop" to what was considered a menial task. Everyone just yearned to sit on Jesus' left and on His right and relax around the table with Him, but not one was willing to be a servant. Notice that the disciples prepared the room because Jesus had asked them to, but no one had asked them to wash feet. Sometimes people will agree to serve when they are asked, but the ministry of the bowl and towel is a spontaneous act of serving.

If one of the disciples had washed the others' feet when they had entered the house, this story would have read very differently. Jesus probably would have beamed, "I want to commend Peter (or James or John) for this demonstration of true spiritual greatness and leadership; this is a perfect example of how I want you to carry on My ministry." But no one rose to the occasion, so Jesus Himself rose to meet the pressing need, which was to wash some grimy feet.

Take the Initiative

I believe that Jesus waited awhile before washing their feet because He was expecting someone to take the initiative.

Initiative is defined as "readiness to embark on bold new ventures; the ability to act first or on one's own, independently of outside influence or control." The lesson we learn from this is that we do not have to wait to be asked to do what needs to be done; as servants, we are free to make decisions and do whatever it takes to get the job done.

- Servants take initiative.

- Servants do not wait for someone else to ask them.

- Servants act spontaneously because they recognize what must be done.

- Servants do what needs doing as soon as possible because that is what servants do.

These disciples whom He had poured His life into had let Him down; none had risen to the occasion or had taken the initiative. He would use their "failure" to reiterate the true attitude found in Kingdom leaders.

This heart of care and serving must not be limited to the local church. Acts of kindness should be performed not just for strangers or our brothers and sisters in Christ, but also for our own families. For example, one day my wife, Bridgette, rushed off to the vet with our sick little dog, Chip. I had just arrived home exhausted after three weeks of ministry and craved a bit of extra sleep, but I got up and cleaned the whole house. Though I often help Bridgette around the house, she was still pleasantly surprised to find it already clean when she came home after three hours at the vet's office. Having assumed that she would have to start tackling all that housework, it was such a blessing to her that I had already done it for her. That is a demonstration of taking the initiative to do what needs doing. A humorous side note concerns a man that I was mentoring at the time. While attending one of my revival meetings at which I related this story, he was so horrified that a man would do housework that he immediately called my wife to find out if it was true!

Jesus was operating contrary to the world's ways because He was a citizen of the Kingdom. The world is selfish, ambitious, proud and arrogant, but Jesus operated in the spirit of humility. He was not just serving but was a servant. He became a servant in His attitude, choosing the way of the bowl and towel.

The world and the Kingdom are at opposite ends. The world says, "get"; the Kingdom says, "give". The world says, "hang on to"; the Kingdom says, "surrender". The world says, "hate"; the Kingdom says, "love" and "forgive". The world says, "greatness is position"; the Kingdom says, "greatness is serving". The world says, "self"; the Kingdom says, "Christ and others". We believers are citizens of the Kingdom. We do not operate as mere men nor do we do what the world does. We are operating at a higher level: by the law of the spirit of life that is in Christ Jesus. We are operating in the law of love that expresses itself in a serving lifestyle.

Every Christian is called to be part of Jesus' ministry team.

The following scriptures make it clear that we are **all** called into the ministry; no one is excluded.

*God has given gifts to **each of you** from his great variety of spiritual gifts. Manage them well so that God's generosity can flow through you.* (1 Peter 4:10 NLT)

I want you to see and remember that "each of you" includes you! We are all given a spiritual gift.

*Having then gifts differing according to the grace that is given to us, **let us use them**: if prophecy, let us prophesy in proportion to our faith; or ministry, let us use it in our ministering; he who teaches, in teaching; he who exhorts, in exhortation; he who gives, with liberality; he* *who leads, with diligence; he who shows mercy, with cheerfulness.* (Romans 12:6-8)

Note that we are to put to use the gifting that has been entrusted to each of us. These gifts are not mere labels or trophies but are meant to be used. In other words, God expects us to flow in the gifts that He gives us.

*And He Himself gave some to be apostles, some prophets, some evangelists, and some pastors and teachers, for the equipping of the saints for the **work of ministry** (the word "ministry" actually means "service"), for the edifying of the body of Christ, till we all come to the unity of the faith and of the knowledge of the Son of God, to a perfect man, to the measure of the stature of the fullness of Christ; that we should no longer be children, tossed to and fro and carried about with every wind of doctrine, by the trickery of men, in the cunning craftiness of deceitful plotting, but, speaking the truth in love, may grow up in all things into Him who is the head--Christ-- from whom the whole body, joined and knit together by what **every joint supplies, according to the effective working by which every part does its share,** causes growth of the body for the edifying of itself in love.* (Ephesians 4:11-16)

Did you catch that? **Every** joint supplies and **every** part is to do its share. Wow! Just imagine if **all** Christians applied this to their lives! Everyone would be involved and committed and a **lot** more would be accomplished.

Set Apart for God

If you are His and your life is devoted to Him, the blood of Jesus has been applied to your life and you are set apart as His vessel. Because you have been born again, you are no longer a sinner but a saint; you do not need to die and be canonized. "Saint" means sanctified, i.e., one set apart for God. Some believers call themselves sinners saved by grace, but you have become a saint because the blood of Jesus has made you worthy to be used as a vessel for God. In the Old Testament, oil was sprinkled upon any object used for worship in the tabernacle or in the temple. This oil was symbolic of the Holy Spirit. The cleansing power of Jesus' blood mixed with the "oil" of the Holy Spirit gives the believer the ability and the authority of God. The blood redeems you and the oil consecrates you. When these are placed upon your life, you are set apart for God. Paul puts it this way:

And He died for all, that those who live should live no longer for themselves, but for Him who died for them and rose again. (2 Corinthians 5:15)

Can you picture what would happen if we actually took this verse to heart and lived no longer for ourselves but for Him? Without a doubt, we would be an unstoppable force in the world! Powerful manifestations of God and multitudes of souls saved would become the norm. I pray for such a day that every believer would live for the glory of God. How can we live for Him? The answer is simple yet profound: by being set apart for Him. And what is implied by being set apart for Him? That we are engaged in the work of ministry.

God must get the firstfruits; that is, He gets the best. Sadly, many Christians either do not give themselves to God or give Him the dregs of their time and finances. Spending the bulk of their time, money, and ability on themselves, their family, and their career, they divide the puny leftovers between the Lord and the ministry of their church. Pastors will tell you that one of their greatest frustrations is the apparent lack of commitment and involvement among their congregants. We are ripe for a revival that will not just make us feel good but will spur us on to **do** good.

The Purpose of Equippers

Ephesians 4 will give us some insight into being a servant. The ascension gift ministries are what I like to call the "equippers."

And He Himself gave some to be apostles, some prophets, some evangelists, and some pastors and teachers. (Ephesians 4:11)

We call these ascension gifts because Jesus has given Himself back to the Church in and through these men and women who are given *"for the equipping of the saints"* (Ephesians 4:12). Equipping ministries prepare the people of God to be effective ministers. They are not called to do all the work of ministry themselves but to impart the truth of God's Word and the vision for the strategic winning of the lost and the growth of the Church. Through their influence, believers should become so inspired and God-filled that they eagerly and enthusiastically engage in the work of God.

The saints are to be brought into maturity, wholeness, health, and stability for the purpose of serving. Four definitions come out of the root word for "equipping":

1. It is "to set a broken bone." Just as a broken bone is set so that the limb can heal and again be used, equippers are to heal broken lives and restore them to usability.

2. Originating from the same Greek word ("katartizo") used for mending the nets, it means to mend lives so that we may harvest the catch. Equippers make us efficient and effective so that we can function according to design. We who have been impacted by God's grace are to attract people to Jesus.

3. It is used to describe the refitting or equipping of a ship so that it may again sail on course. Equippers train us so that our destiny in God is fulfilled. We are to be equipped or refitted so that we may sail the oceans of life and ministry to bring many to salvation.

4. It means to be radically adjusted. Equippers radically adjust us in order to bring us into God's order and balance.

Change Must Come

These days it is hard to find discipling or equipping churches; instead, we have meeting-driven and program-driven churches. Often, these meetings and programs are designed to keep Christians busy and happy rather than to equip and train them. Many churches today are focused on man rather than focused on God and what He has called us to do. Pulpit ministry has taken precedence over discipleship, with few being personally taught and trained. Too many know the Word of God academically yet are having negligible impact in the vision for winning the lost and growing the local church. It is time for change. We need to get back to the Great Commission to make disciples.

I would like to bring challenge to all apostles, prophets, evangelists, pastors, and teachers to become equippers of the saints. Their ministry should birth servants (ministers), not just a Christian audience that merely attends meetings. As equippers invest their lives for the mobilization of the entire Body of Christ into effective and anointed ministry, we will see the equipped bring in the harvest of souls. When these gifts function according to the intention of God, the power of God will be released and the Church will grow. The huge shift that must take place will start with the ascension ministries which will in turn birth other ministries.

Two thousand years ago, the Lord was adding to the Church daily those who were being saved (Acts 2:47), and today He still desires to add to the Church **daily**. If the Church has not grown as He would like, I suggest that it is due to the indifference to the call to ministry by much of the Body of Christ. We need to create an environment conducive for God to grow the Church, and that environment is one of equipped and inspired ministries. I would recommend to pastors that rather than trying to grow your congregation, grow the people to be strong in the Word, in passion, in vision, in love, and in anointing. As they are equipped and trained for ministry (service) and begin to function, it will follow naturally that the congregation will begin to grow. When every joint supplies and every part does its share, both numerical and qualitative growth will result. All Christians ought to be exposed to an equipping ministry to awaken their hearts to their purpose, which is to serve God, humanity, and the Church.

I also want to challenge every believer to become wide open to God by going beyond the traditional church attendee mentality and getting equipped for the work of ministry. Because of this audience mentality, few souls are being saved, few ministries are being released, and volunteerism in the local church is at an all-time low. We have too many jobs to be done and too few people to do them. As Jesus said, "The harvest is ripe but the laborers are few." Nothing has changed from that time until today; we still need servant-hearted workers to be equipped and released into the work of ministry. After we pray that the Lord of the harvest sends forth laborers, we should then report for duty in answer to our own prayer.

Statistics show that the Body of Christ is dysfunctional.

"Dysfunctional" means impaired or abnormal in function, especially of a bodily system or social group.

A number of years ago my youngest son was stricken with a disease that left him paralyzed from the waist down. When I saw him lying in his hospital bed with only a fraction of his body working, I got a glimpse of the dysfunctional Body of Christ. It is dysfunctional, because only 20% is working according to the design of God, which is that every believer be a functioning member. In less than two weeks, my son was healed and raised from his bed of affliction by the power of God. Just as he was raised up and made whole, I believe with all my heart that God will heal the Body of Christ, so that every member becomes a passionate servant doing all His will. A revival is coming that will empower believers to become functional, to be whole and able to walk in power and ministry.

Statistics confirm my observation that only about 20% of Christians actively serve in their churches. Where your treasure is, there you will find your heart

(Luke 12:34), so those who love the Church and the God of the Church will invest their life and energy into its function and vision. On the other hand, those whose hearts are not in the Church or its mission will not give themselves to the work of God. Such people have been birthed into a salvation that takes them from hell to heaven but includes no sense of obligation to impact this generation. There is nothing wrong with the desire to avoid hell, but God leaves us on earth so that we can represent Him and carry out His agenda while we are here. As His ambassadors, we are to be engaged in the priorities of heaven.

If 80% of the members of a local church are not functioning, that body is surely dysfunctional! Every joint supplies and every part does its share (Ephesians 4:16), so if every part does not do its share and every joint does not supply, the body is crippled. The astounding figure of 80% of the Body of Christ not functioning is utterly unacceptable. If 80% of your body were to shut down, you would need a doctor immediately. In the same way, today's Church is in dire need of resuscitation, because 80% is not functioning according to its design. (Let me point out that throughout this book, I use "church" to refer to the local church, and "Church" to refer to the wider body, the Body of Christ.)

I believe that 10% of Christians are active (this is known as the core group); 10% are partially or sporadically active (they participate at times but not at the level of full commitment); and 80% are inactive (by and large, these are the Sunday Christians). The latter group may live right and live morally, but so do many secular-minded people and cultists. Morality and behavior are not sufficient to impact this generation; while morality is certainly preferable to immorality, Christians are destined to be people of vision, passion, zeal, and anointing. Our goal is for **every** Christian to be a passionate, anointed minister, each one engaged in the work of God.

Napoleon was once walking around the front lines checking on his soldiers, when he came upon a soldier asleep at his post. Taking the soldier's weapon, he stood guard until the soldier woke up. Can you imagine the soldier's shocked face when he awoke to see Napoleon standing there in his post, carrying out what was the soldier's responsibility? Today, Jesus is walking around the front lines and finding many Christians asleep on duty. They are not engaged in the holy operations of the Spirit nor fulfilling the work of ministry. Even if the equippers are committed to equipping the saints, the saints must also be committed to being the ministers they are equipped to be.

Jesus is coming for a glorious Church, so we are in a period of transition. We (the equippers) are taking our role and you (the ministers) are taking yours. You are called to the work of ministry; we are called to minister to you by serving your life through the grace gift given us to equip you to carry His name and His power to the world.

We, as equippers, should not be satisfied until you are all equipped ministers who are making a difference. When that happens, the Church grows up and grows big. In other words, when we do our part and you do your part, maturity will be evident, and with maturity will come consistent numerical growth. When churches and people cease to grow, it means that we are not doing our job and you are not doing yours. Every believer must become a minister. None should be unemployed or sit on the sidelines, because it is time for **everyone** to be engaged in the work of God, both in the local church as well as outside in the world.

In summary:

- All Christians have been uniquely gifted to represent God to the lost and to serve in their church. We are not just saved to go to heaven but to serve God and the Body of Christ on earth.

- Many Christians are not functioning according to the grace gifts of God. Despite knowing that there is a plan for their lives, they sit on the sidelines as spectators rather than participants. Such passivity will lead to frustration and a lukewarm heart.

- Jesus actively served His disciples, demonstrating that "ministry" is really about doing what needs to be done. No task is too menial or insignificant.

- Jesus is our model; since He was a servant, we must become servants also. True greatness and spiritual leadership are best expressed through a serving heart.

Questions:

Why did Jesus wash the disciples feet?

Why did Jesus wait until supper was underway to wash their feet?

Why do you think that the disciples did not do what was required?

We read "that those who live should live no longer for themselves, but for Him who died for them and rose again" (2 Corinthians 5:15).

What does it mean not to live for yourself but for Him?

Have you been living for yourself? In what ways?

What can you do to change this? Will you make these changes?

When you think of ministry, what do you think of?

Do you see yourself as a minister?

Imagine that you were a disciple at that supper. Do you think that you would have washed the feet of the guests as they entered the house?

Would you say that you have been a spectator or a participant?

At Jesus' time, foot washing was considered a menial task that no one wanted to do. What tasks today can you think of that would be considered menial?

What is your attitude toward serving someone that you don't particularly care for? Is your attitude different when you serve someone you like better?

Chapter 2

Serving from the Position of Wholeness

I have a saying that goes like this, "If you serve without being a servant, you are an offense waiting to happen." Over the many years that I have been in the pastorate, I have found that good people who serve without having the attitude of a servant are often candidates for becoming disenfranchised or offended. They are zealous to be involved but do not minister out of balance and wholeness but from their need:

- Need for appreciation
- Need for recognition
- Need for promotion
- Need for acceptance

Those who engage in the work of ministry should have the right attitude, i.e., the attitude of a servant. Without this, they will become easily offended and their involvement will be short-lived. It will not be long before they withdraw into "attendance mode," swelling the ranks of the uninvolved. Even worse, they may leave the church and return to the world, placing all the blame on the pastor or the church. In reality, the problem was not the pastor but that their lives were not whole. Their intention to do something for God was fleeting because their feelings were hurt:

- They felt used or abused.

- They felt unappreciated or underappreciated.

- They never got out of it what they felt they deserved.

An Offense Waiting to Happen

Well-meaning Christians who are emotionally wounded or insecure in their identity will eventually get offended when they serve because they are not servants in their heart.

There is a huge difference between serving and being a servant. One is something you **do** and the other is someone you **are**. We are human beings and not human doings. If we are not secure in our being, we will never be good in our doing. When believers go through the motions of serving but are not servant-hearted, you will discover that they have an expectation, usually for some form of recognition or promotion. When they do not receive what they feel is coming to them, they can get mean and nasty. That which was to have been a blessing, producing fruit and reward for them, has instead produced discontentment. Feeling cheated or victimized, they can become vicious, because they served with ulterior motives.

Such people are not broken in the biblical way (having a broken and contrite heart) but are only "broken" emotionally or psychologically. Having unrealistic expectations, they either get offended or end up offending someone else. They are not operating out of security and order but out of their own need: a need to be wanted, to be promoted, to be appreciated. In contrast, those who serve that are secure in who they are (their new creation identity) and where they are going (their new creation vision and purpose) will one day be greeted with those prized words from the Lord, "Well done, good and faithful servant."

Jesus was established in wholeness:

And supper being ended, the devil having already put it into the heart of Judas Iscariot, Simon's son, to betray Him, Jesus, **knowing that the Father had given all things into His hands, and that He had come from God and was going to God***....* (John 13:2-3)

Jesus was a very secure and emotionally whole man:

- He did not serve to be recognized.

- He did not serve to be promoted (even though those who serve will be promoted).

- He did not serve because He was insecure.

- He did not serve out of false humility but was genuinely humble.

- He did not look for position.

- He did not feel inferior.

- He did not put on a mask or false front.
- He did not have any ulterior motives.

His motives were pure because:

- He was secure.
- He knew who He was.
- He knew where He came from.
- He knew where He was going.
- He was at peace with Himself.
- He was at peace with His Father.

Jesus was whole:

- He was never flustered.
- He was never pressured by anything around Him.
- He was walking in perfect unison with God.

Being totally secure and whole, Jesus did not feel degraded by washing dirty feet. He was as comfortable doing that as He was preaching, teaching, casting out demons, or healing the sick. He was not offended by the omission of the disciples but used the occasion to demonstrate that the greatness of leading was not in position or title but in the heart of a servant.

Take off the outer garments and take up the tools of a servant.

Jesus *"rose from supper and laid aside His garments"* (John 13:4). In order to serve, you have to lay aside certain things:

- Your personal agenda
- Your own needs
- Your will and methods
- Your pride and reputation

People who serve others should become like those four friends who carried the paralyzed man to the house where Jesus was visiting. To get that man to Jesus, they had to lose focus of their own journey; they had to forget about their time constraints and where they could have been in the time it took to help him. Some of the four may even have had physical needs of their own, but they laid these aside to meet the needs of someone else. In so doing they served their friend.

We are all busy with things to do; we all have priorities and important matters that require our attention. The difference is that servants will lay these aside to meet the needs of someone else. Jesus laid aside His garments.

Definition of a Servant

"Doulos," the Greek word for servant, means "one who serves another even to the disregard of his own needs and interests."

People move to the United States in hopes of enjoying a better quality of life. We are a thriving nation with lots of rights and privileges that are unknown in many parts of the world, yet we also have responsibilities. For example, we must pay taxes and abide by the laws of the land in order to enjoy our benefits. The fact that we have rights and privileges does not negate our responsibilities. Similarly, as citizens of the Kingdom of God, we have rights and privileges but also responsibilities. In order to do God's will, we will have to lay aside those rights and privileges. Perhaps we could sit at the table and be waited upon, but instead, we choose to carry the bowl and towel. It is not forced upon us but is our decision.

At times you may be asked to do something in the church and, of course, your response should be, "Yes, I will." There is also spontaneous serving, and that happens when you see a need and fill it. Both opportunities should be embraced with a serving heart. Though some people will only do something when asked, you should not wait for this because the Bible says, *"Whatever your hand finds to do, do it with your might"* (Ecclesiastes 9:10). That is the response of a servant. Jesus was neither asked nor commanded to serve, but He freely chose to do so. The greatest mark of a servant is spontaneous serving, i.e., seeing the need and simply doing what needs to be done.

Serving Jesus by Serving Others

When someone comes to you and says, "We need this to be done," you should do it willingly, cheerfully, and generously. When your pastor stands up and says, "We need workers in this area," it is actually Jesus making this plea. If you could see Jesus standing there, it would dramatically affect you. If Jesus stood up on Sunday morning and said, "We need three volunteers for the nursery," 300 people would instantly come forward to respond, inspired to action because they could see Jesus.

The reason that many Christians do not serve the Lord is that they do not see Jesus; instead, they see a man or they see a job that needs doing. After all, there is always someone else who will do the work. These people need spiritual surgery on their eyes. "I am just doing it for the kids." No, you are not just doing it for the kids; you are actually doing it for Jesus. You are not doing it for the pastor but for "Pastor Jesus." There is One standing behind your pastor and that is the Chief Shepherd, Jesus. He can ask you and He can require certain things of you. If He is your Lord, you should always say, "Yes, Lord." Even if it causes inconvenience, servants always respond positively because there is no such thing as "No, Lord."

Jesus took the bowl and towel and girded Himself. After that, He poured water into a basin and began to wash the disciples' feet, and to wipe them with the towel with which He was girded. (John 13:5)

This was an act of true humility, true wholeness, and yet total brokenness in that He was fully yielded to the things of God. There was no ambition, no pride, no arrogance, but rather purity of heart, motive, and soul. This is the greatest example of a servant that we could ever see.

Washing Feet in Church

Then He came to Simon Peter. And Peter said to Him, "Lord, are You washing my feet?' Jesus answered and said to him, "What I am doing you do not understand now, but you will know after this." Peter said to Him, "You shall never wash my feet!" Jesus answered him, "If I do not wash you, you have no part with Me." Simon Peter said to Him, "Lord, not my feet only, but also my hands and my head!" Jesus said to him, 'He who is bathed needs only to wash his feet, but is completely clean; and you are clean, but not all of you." For He knew who would betray Him; therefore He said, "You are not all clean." So when He had washed their feet, taken His garments, and sat down again, He said to them, "Do you know what I have done to you? You call Me teacher and Lord, and you say well, for so I am. If I then, your Lord and Teacher, have washed your feet, you also ought to wash one another's feet. For I have given you an example, that you should do as I have done to you. Most assuredly, I say to you, a servant is not greater than his master; nor is he who is sent greater than he who sent him. If you know these things, blessed are you if you do them. (John 13:6-17)

Jesus demonstrated what being a servant looked like. I am not against "foot washing" in church, for this simple practice can have tremendous healing potential. One of the greatest ways to heal strife in relationships is to come with a bowl and towel and to wash feet.

Jesus said, *"If I then, your Lord and Teacher, have washed your feet,* **you also ought to wash one another's feet***"* (John 13:14). Based on these words, some churches practice foot washing because they consider it to be an ordinance in addition to water baptism and the Lord's Supper. Though I have no problem with foot washing in the church, per se, sometimes we take what is meant to be practical and then gird it in religiosity because it feels good to our senses.

Foot washing in church can be very meaningful. I have seen this practice bring healing to broken relationships as well as renew love and respect for leadership and for one another. Broken relationships can be healed in the demonstration of what Jesus did, but the reality is that it is easy to wash feet in church and make it a part of our service. We can even make it a tradition that we go through once a year or every so often, yet this tradition can wind up obscuring what we were actually meant to be doing.

In today's church, the practice of foot washing makes me smile, if not laugh. To avoid any embarrassment, people come to the service with feet already clean and pedicured. The worst thing that could happen would be to find that in your haste to arrive at church on time, you put on mismatched socks. (I also wonder what the ladies do when wearing pantyhose. This could be awkward!) How different from olden days when this practice served a real purpose!

I believe that what Jesus was demonstrating was not intended to be turned into an ordinance in a church service but was to be done as a way of life. He was saying, "You have to live like this because this is true leadership and true ministry; it is all about meeting whatever need is facing others at the moment." Whether the need is practical or spiritual does not matter; both require us to strip off, take up, and wash, doing whatever needs to be done. It is not to become a ritual during a church service but is something that we do automatically as a way of life.

Serving opens the way for the gospel.

In the African nation of Malawi some years ago, one of our missionary workers came across a child who had fallen into a fire and had severely burned his leg, foot, and elbow. The child's mother swept him up in her arms to rush him to the nearest clinic, but sadly, he was sent home without any medication or treatment because the clinic had no burn kits for his wounds.

We had tried to work in this village before this incident, but the gospel could not go forth because the chief had forbidden us to preach in his jurisdiction. The missionary used whatever medical ointments and bandages he had in his vehicle that could at least try to protect the wound and stop any infection from setting in. When he got back to his house and called the United States to share the incident, I arranged for sufficient burn kits to be sent overnight. This was a costly endeavor, but in the light of the cost of our salvation, it was not too much to pay to bring God's healing to that family.

With the burn kits in hand, our missionary would travel over dirt roads for seventeen miles every day for several weeks. The infection was prevented and soon the child's wounds started to heal. Thanks to the missionary's creativity, compassion, and some medical skills, the child's leg and arm were restored to full use. But that is not the miracle.

The miracle came when the witch doctor in the area became infuriated that our missionary was found working in the village and had then reported this to the chief. The child's mother came to our defense, stressing that the hospital had no medicines and no one in the village could help them, but this missionary had gone out of his way at a fairly high expense to save her child. Putting herself at risk, she chased the witch doctor away from her home and confronted the chief. This so touched the chief's heart that since that day, our teams were allowed to preach in that village and many were won to the Lord. Compassion and a serving attitude, together with the gospel, brought dramatic change, not only to the child but to the village. And that is the ministry of the bowl and towel.

Foot washing filled a practical need.

For us today, it is easier to bring a bowl and a towel to church and to wash people's feet than to go and wash their car, paint the house of a single mom or mow her grass. Inside the four walls of the church it feels spiritual, but out there it is just plain old work. Jesus did not wash the disciples' feet as a symbolic act; rather, it was a practical act that simply met the need of that moment. Of course, we love to turn everything in the church into bells and smells, frills and thrills, but the fact is that Jesus washed dirty, stinking feet.

What Jesus modeled was not meant to become a religious act within the confines of a church, but was meant to be something done by servants to help people in their need. He said, *"I have given you an example, that you should do as I have done to you"* (John 13:15). Far from doing it just to make a point, He did it because it needed to be done, and then that became an example for us. He continued, *"If you know these things, blessed are you if you do them"* (John 13:17). So if you know what is good and you do it, you are blessed.

Jesus was teaching us to be willing to meet people at their point of need in a practical way, which in fact is spiritual as well. It is not just a practical thing but it is a holy work that is done unto the Lord. Though washing a car is just work, when you help that person who does not have time to do it or you go to a widow to clean or paint her house, you are actually demonstrating Jesus to them, believer or unbeliever. Whether we are doing acts of kindness to believers or unbelievers, we are demonstrating Jesus to them.

In summary:

- When those who are not whole get busy in the work of God, they will often become offended. The offense might be caused by something as simple as the pastor not saying thank you, and thus, they feel taken for granted.

- Jesus was secure because He was whole. His wholeness allowed Him to attend to any and all situations, whether these involved demons, sickness, hungry people, or dirty feet.

- Because Jesus knew His position and identity, He did not need to resort to finding acceptance in man's applause or recognition. Everything He did was done not for promotion or recognition but simply because it was what servants did.

- Foot washing should not be turned into a religious ceremony in church but should translate into doing something practical to help or meet a need.

Questions:

In what ways did Jesus serve? Give specific examples.

When church leadership asks for help in a particular area:

- What is your immediate reaction?

- What goes through your mind?

- Do you volunteer or do you wait to be asked personally?

- Would your reaction be different, if Jesus Himself were the one asking for the help? Explain.

After washing the disciples' feet, Jesus said, *"I have given you an example, that you should do as I have done to you"* (John 13:15). What lesson was Jesus modeling when He washed the disciples' feet?

Since Jesus was secure and emotionally whole, He didn't serve to be recognized, applauded, or promoted.

- Have you had ulterior motives for serving?

- Have you ever served to be recognized, applauded, or promoted?

- What sort of recognition would you like to receive for serving?

- Have you ever expected to receive some sort of recognition?

- Did you get it? If you didn't, how did it make you feel?

- Have you ever felt a need for others to know that you are serving?

- Would you serve if no one else knew about it?

- When you have served, have you ever felt superior to others in some way?

Did Jesus receive any recognition for the acts of kindness that He performed? Explain.

If people serve but are not secure in their identity, what can happen?

When leadership in church talks about a need and asks for help, do you volunteer or do you wait to be asked?

What goes through your mind?

Do you wait for someone to ask you to do something, or do you take the initiative when you see a need?

Can you think of an instance when you took the initiative to fill a need rather than waiting to be asked?

Can you think of some practical ways in which you could serve:

- your spouse?

- your brothers and sisters at church?

- your colleagues at work?

- the needy?

10% of Christians are active. (This is known as the core group.) 10% are partially or sporadically active. (They participate at times, but not at the level of full commitment.) 80% of Christians are inactive.

Which group are you in? Why?

In what ways have other people served you?

Were you grateful?

Did you take it for granted?

Well Done...good and faithful servant

> Did they expect anything in return?
>
>
> How do you feel when others serve you? Uncomfortable? Undeserving?

Chapter 3

Not All who Serve are Servants

We do not serve for personal gain but rather to give and to ease the load of someone else. We engage in the work that is before us because we are servants, not because it is forced upon us. Some offended people will say, "But I have been serving in this area for three years and no one has ever thanked me or recognized me; what should I do?" Such disappointed people have been serving faithfully and diligently, but unlike true servants, they did not abandon their all but served with the expectation of reward.

True servants, as opposed to people who are busy doing the work, have no expectation other than to bring pleasure to the heart of God by doing His will. These servants will say "Thank you" to God. Their pleasure comes from knowing that they did what He called them to do. They are comfortable as doorkeepers in the house of the Lord and can do it for the rest of their days because menial tasks are not a pressure or burden but rather a joy and a delight. These true servants are operating out of wholeness.

Martha and Mary

Now it happened as they went that He entered a certain village; and a certain woman named Martha welcomed Him into her house. And she had a sister called Mary, who also sat at Jesus' feet and heard His word. But

Martha was distracted with much serving, and she approached Him and said, "Lord, do You not care that my sister has left me to serve alone? Therefore tell her to help me." And Jesus answered and said to her, "Martha, Martha, you are worried and troubled about many things. But one thing is needed, and Mary has chosen that good part, which will not be taken away from her." (Luke 10:38-42)

Martha and Mary were the sisters of Lazarus. Martha was probably the eldest of the family, and since the residence is called "her house," some believe that she was a widow and that Mary and Lazarus lived with her in Bethany. She seems to have been of an anxious, bustling spirit, eager to be helpful in providing the best things for the Master's use.

In contrast, Mary wanted to take advantage of the opportunity to sit at Jesus' feet, gleaning from His life and message. I do not believe for one minute that she was lazy but simply chose to soak in His presence. No doubt Martha also respected the Lord and desired to draw from His life, but she saw a need to be involved in the practical responsibilities of hosting this revered guest. We can almost visualize the scenario: Initially excited about the privilege of cooking and caring for this famous rabbi, Martha now began to fume as she heard Mary laughing and enjoying herself at His feet. Like a pressure cooker, her irritation bubbled to the point that she had to let off steam. Banging down a plate and glaring at her sister, she cried out, "Lord! Command Mary to come to the kitchen and help me."

Martha was absorbed, preoccupied, and distracted, while Mary was focused exclusively on Jesus. Paul might have had a picture of Martha in mind when he spoke of serving the Lord "without distraction":

I am saying this for your benefit, not to place restrictions on you. I want you to do whatever will help you serve the Lord best, with as few distractions as possible. (1 Corinthians 7:35 NLT)

Notice that Jesus does not rebuke Mary for her inactivity but neither does He rebuke Martha; instead, He gently encourages her to serve from the place of peace and joy. It appears that Martha's serving was not done with the attitude of a servant. From having met Martha's relatives over my years in ministry, I will say that though they are busy and active, too often they serve with a huge attitude and invariably complain about those who should be helping them. This does not mean that a lack of involvement or laziness and indifference are to be condoned, but grumbling while serving is just as bad as not serving. Servants should not whine or complain because servants serve. If you serve and are not a servant, you are just an offense waiting to happen. "Woe is me! I alone have to look after the children. Where are all the mothers?" and so the list of complaints could go on.

People who serve should remember this verse:

Don't be selfish; don't try to impress others. Be humble, thinking of others as better than yourselves. (Philippians 2:3, NLT)

Worship precedes service.

Remember this vital principle: worship always precedes service. Since all service must flow out of our relationship with Jesus, we will find ourselves becoming irritated or even offended if we serve without having spent time at His feet. We will start pouting, "I alone have been left with this work." "I am being used." "I am not going to volunteer anymore because it all falls on my shoulders." "Why are so few helping me?" When we allow this to happen, we become bitter (as Martha did) and eventually back away from serving in the future.

We need to become a combination of a Mary and a Martha, because such people know how to sit at the feet of Jesus and also know how to get some work done.

We worship God and serve man.

"Therefore, if You will worship before me, all will be Yours." And Jesus answered and said to him, "Get behind Me, Satan! For it is written, 'You shall worship the LORD your God, and Him only you shall serve.'" (Luke 4:7-8)

As believers, worship of God is our first responsibility. However, since it is so much easier to simply close our eyes and worship than to be busy serving Him, many who are found singing in church on Sunday remain uninvolved with suffering humanity or in helping out in the church. Our reasonable worship or service is to present ourselves a living sacrifice (Romans 12:1), so those who are going to serve God by touching humanity will live sacrificially. It is not just about being in church and singing songs but it is about touching humanity in the place of need.

In declaring, *"You shall worship the LORD your God, and Him only you shall serve"* (Luke 4:8), Jesus delineated our two responsibilities toward God: worship and service.

Often in the Old Testament, the word "worship" refers to servitude. Jesus says, "Him only you shall serve." The word "serve" literally means to "minister to; to render religious service or homage, to worship; to worship God in the observance of the rites instituted for His worship."

Thus, every Christian is called to worship God and to be a servant. When you are in right standing with Him, you will have a heart to win and serve man, because a true worshiper will have a love for humanity. You cannot be right with God without wanting to touch man. Anyone who becomes spiritually minded wants to flow from the tender heart of God toward humanity and do something to advance the Kingdom, to build the Church, to reach souls, and to minister to the weak.

Carnal people have the heart of man, always looking to see what they can get out of something, but worshippers are servants of God who live to be a blessing and help others. Unless you are a worshiper, you will get so busy trying to deal with the multitude of needs that the weight of the load will overwhelm you. Jesus said, *"Take My yoke upon you...For My yoke is easy and My burden is light"* (Matthew 11:29-30).

What we receive on the mountaintop must then touch others.

When Jesus took Peter, James, and John up on a high mountain, the glory of God came down and they watched as Jesus was transfigured before their very eyes (Matthew 17:1-18). Then Moses and Elijah appeared and spoke with Him. What an extraordinary time in the glory this must have been for these disciples. Peter told Jesus that he would build tabernacles for Him, Moses, and Elijah. He was so overcome by the intensity of this encounter that he just wanted to stay in it. And who could blame him? After all, who would want to leave during such holy times? However, the fact of the matter is that desperate people with desperate needs were waiting in the valley below. As glorious as this time on the mountain was, there came a time to go back down to the place of pouring out from the deposit that they had received in the presence of God.

It is wonderful to be in the glory of God on the mountaintop enjoying close fellowship with the Lord, but then we need to take what we have received down to the valley below and set people free with it. We are carriers of the deposit of God; what we get is for us but more importantly, it is to flow through us to someone else. The imparted glory from the mountaintop is released through us into the people in the valley. We are to serve humanity from the abundance of what we have received. Jesus put it very simply: *"Freely you have received, freely give"* (Matthew 10:8). We are not confined to serving people out of our limited ability and provision, but we operate as conduits of the eternal and abundant supply of God. As our lives are transformed and conformed to His image while we bask in His presence, we must take responsibility to minister to the valley below.

Keeping Your Heart Tender

Without having a heart of worship toward God, you will eventually start to neglect your relationship with Him and try to compensate by the busyness of your spiritual activities. If you do not stay right with God, you do not stay right with man; you get so busy that you hide behind that thing, whether it be the sound board, the musical instruments, the pulpit, the children, the nursery, etc. You are so busy doing spiritual tasks, but you are not spiritual. Given enough time, something will offend you and you will explode. What in the past was pleasant will soon become an offense. You may become judgmental or aggressive toward the one that you are trying to help. You may lose the sweetness of your spirit, because your walk with God is not where it should be and your priorities are messed up. You can get so busy serving man and so wrapped up in the activities of the church that your first love passion for the Lord is lost. When the work of ministry becomes your top priority, you can lose the love for the Lord of the work. It is of the utmost importance to stay in the place of worship, because it is the worship of God that will keep your service toward man pure and sweet. Worship keeps the Lord in His rightful place as #1 and keeps the work in its rightful place, all to the glory of God.

Much church strife is caused by people who have lost their relationship with God; they then take the position of judge, jury, and executioner. Worship will keep you in the place of submission because you must humble yourself in order to worship. Worship changes you and conforms you to the image of God because you become like the one you worship. You become more Godlike in your nature.

Staying in right relationship with God will keep your motives pure and your attitude right. When you are busy serving but do not get what you want out of it, you start to grumble, complain, and get an attitude. You cannot give to man without first giving to God, so if you would just stay right with Him, it will be so much easier to stay right with man.

People who are involved in a serving role should operate from the attitude of a servant. In other words, you should serve because that is what servants do...serve! If you serve but are not a servant in attitude, you will gripe about those who do not give, pray, or volunteer. However, since being involved is not forced labor as in a concentration camp, there is no need to be concerned with who is not involved. Serving is a voluntary role that we choose because we love the Lord and His people. We do not demand thanks, recognition or promotion, and we do not fear punishment or rejection. We serve merely because that is what we are called to do, period.

Those who volunteer to be involved in a position in the church should approach their responsibility with the attitude of a servant. Whether fulfilling a leadership role or doing a simple chore, they need to be humble servants in motive and attitude.

- There is no place for power-hungry people.
- There is no place for people with hidden agendas.
- There is no place for people who are going to grumble and complain about those who are not

serving or about those who are serving alongside them.

- There is no place for selfish ambition or vanity.

Whether you are asked to be involved or you offer your services, you should approach your position with the desire to glorify God and bless others. You should never cop an attitude when you see yourself sacrificing while others like Mary just sit at the feet of Jesus. Ideally, everyone should be a combination of Mary and Martha (at least a Martha that does not complain). Everyone should be a worshipper who longs to sit at Jesus' feet. In fact, all service must follow a worshiping heart, as it is written, *"You shall worship the LORD your God, and Him only shall you serve"* (Matthew 4:10).

All believers should be involved within the church and on the outside as well, serving sacrificially to help someone else. We should all be engaged in the reaching of the lost and the growth and development of the Body of Christ. We have been gifted for this cause:

As each one has received a gift, **minister** *it to one another, as good stewards of the manifold grace of God.* (1 Peter 4:10)

"Diakoneo," the Greek word for "minister," means "to attend to, to serve, to wait upon."

Notice the following:

- "As **each one** has received a gift" means that **you** have been uniquely gifted by God.

- Through this gift you are to serve (or minister to) someone else.

- You ought to be a good steward of this gift, meaning that you should diligently use it for the growth and development of the local church.

Gifted to Serve

Among the various motivational gifts listed in Romans 12 is the gift of serving.

Having then gifts differing according to the grace that is given to us, let us use them: if prophecy, let us prophesy in proportion to our faith; ***or ministry, let us use it in our ministering****; he who teaches, in teaching; he who exhorts, in exhortation; he who gives, with liberality; he who leads, with diligence; he who shows mercy, with cheerfulness.* (Romans 12:6-8)

Another version states this as follows:

We have different gifts, according to the grace given us. If a man's gift is prophesying, let him use it in proportion to his faith. ***If it is serving, let him serve.*** (Romans 12:6-7 NIV)

Let me address the difference between being uniquely gifted by God and just doing what needs to be done. As you know, all of us are called to pray, to give, and to evangelize, yet some people are especially called and gifted in these areas. In the same way, all of us are called to serve, but some are uniquely gifted to serve. There are those who open their homes and do their best to take good care of their guests, but others are particularly gifted in being hospitable. For example, my friends Roger and Mary Jane always host me in their beautiful home when I am preaching in Bloomington. Besides being very sensitive to my needs, they are truly gifted in hospitality. Every area of their home is organized and spotless. They want their home to be comfortable and a suitable environment for me to work and rest. They go out of their way to look after me, preparing meals that seem to ensure that I always leave a "bigger man" than when I arrived. I usually pick up a few pounds, thanks to after-meeting ice creams, peach cobblers, and a nonstop supply of coffee. Though, as believers, they ought to be hospitable, they are "gifted" by God to be hospitable.

While God has called all believers to be servants, not everyone is "gifted" to be a servant. The gift of serving goes beyond sheer will power and the determination to fulfill one's Christian responsibility. Those with this gift are motivated into service by a divine enablement that causes them to flourish and thrive in serving.

Not one Christian is excluded from being gifted by God; each has received a divine deposit or enablement from Him (1 Peter 4:10). Every Christian is called to be a part of the ministry team. Mike Petzer, a good friend who pastors a church in Tucson, says to those being welcomed into membership, "Welcome into the ministry." Most pastors will say, "Welcome into membership," but Mike has taken this to another level by choosing to raise up ministers. His goal is to build a congregation of servant-hearted followers of Jesus rather than an audience that sits back and watches a handful of ministers at work. Every Christian is either gifted as a servant or becomes a servant, and every local church should be a place to equip its members to be servants (ministers).

Do you serve or are you a servant?

God does not want you simply to serve in your church but rather to be a servant in heart and attitude. When disappointment and offense inevitably come, those who are engaged in serving but are not servants will most likely explode, have a hissy fit or simply bury the pain and anger and become bitter. In contrast, having laid down their rights and personal agendas, servants do not blow up when pressure comes. Having taken up the bowl and the towel, they are dead to self and alive to God. They have their eyes fixed on the Master and their hands to the plow…or the bowl and towel…or the toilet brush. They are not seeking recognition or promotion but rather they live for Christ.

A woman enthusiastically tells her pastor, "Pastor, God spoke to me and has called me to help in the nursery." She goes into the nursery: "Oh, I just love the little darlings; these are the future Billy Grahams, Smith Wigglesworths, and John G. Lakes. I am going to bless them, pray for them, and help them become great in God. I am going to invest into their little lives."

By the end of the morning, while the rest of the church has been shouting and dancing and celebrating in the sanctuary, this woman has gotten smelly hands, baby puke on her shoulder, and a pile of dirty diapers. This was not how she envisioned it would be, and she is mad! Making Billy Grahams is harder than she thought. "Pastor, I have a revelation! God said to me, 'Well done, good and faithful servant'; I can now enter into the prophetic. God has called me to be an intercessor to your ministry." Do you see what has happened? People have a romantic notion about what serving is all about; it appears to be so fulfilling but after a few short months the glamour has worn off and it becomes good old-fashioned hard work.

Whether working in the nursery, cleaning, sound, worship or administration, there will always be an incident or excuse to trigger offense. Someone who should have been on duty with you does not arrive. Suddenly you have to improvise and things are not going according to plan. Frustration sets in and your eyes are no longer fixed on the Master but on the flaws in the system and the lack of expected support. In such situations, you must remain faithful and diligent, being patient in enduring these weaknesses and flaws. The fact is that the more involved you are in your church, the more aware you are of what is going on and what the needs are. You get to see both the good and the evil.

There **will** be little Billy Grahams in the making, but they will have dirty diapers and runny noses. If you get into greeting or ushering, you are going to find rude people. There will be imperfections, because the Body of Christ is under God's construction and development. We will always have young, growing Christians as well as mature, mean old Christians. We will have prodigals who come home and we will have elder brothers who are upset.

Servants do not quit.

Because all kinds of people make up the Body, you will have to understand that in your serving you will see the best of people and the worst of them. If you quit because you see the worst, you are not a servant but you are just going through the motions of serving. Servants serve in spite of the circumstances. It has been said that pain is inevitable but misery is optional, so if you feel let down, get over it. At some point, there will be disappointment when you serve, but allowing misery and offense to become a root of bitterness is your decision.

Servants serve without condition because they have abandoned themselves. They are submitted to godly leadership and serve whether they agree or disagree.

When you say, "Well, I would not do it that way," that is when submission kicks in. Submission is not submission until you submit. Similarly, obedience is obedience when you obey.

Pastors should be wary when congregants write letters, "Dear Pastor, I have been ministered to by God, and I want to tell you I am committed, I am submitted, I am going to serve your ministry." It is one thing to write this on paper but quite another to have it written in your heart. My experience has taught me that after several weeks, many of these same people will be writing letters to a different tune: "Dear pastor, you have blessed my life in a wonderful way, **but** (there is always a big bold "but" in these letters) I am resigning because God is leading me to serve in a different church." This is "Christianese" for "I am offended because I never got enough out of the exchange." You don't have to write letters or tell the pastor how devoted you are to serving. As the Nike ad says, "Just do it!"

In summary:

- Above all else comes our worship of God, and then out of that love relationship flows our service to man. Maintaining this order will keep our spirit sweet.

- The goal is not simply to be engaged in serving activities but to become a servant. Servants serve because that is who they are. We are not human doings but human beings. When we discover our being, i.e., who we are in Christ, we can successfully and sacrificially do.

- We do not want to choose between being either a Martha or a Mary but want something of each of them. We want to be a Mary, because we understand the priority of sitting at the feet of Jesus, and we also want to serve like Martha (but without her resentful attitude).

- We are servants and therefore we serve. We do not merely serve but we are servants in heart and attitude. That is what we do when we are servants…we serve.

Questions:

What is the difference between a servant and someone who serves?

Ideally, should you be a Martha, a Mary, or both?
Which are you? A Mary? A "happy" Martha? Both?

Why do you think Jesus did not rebuke Mary for her inactivity?

With what kind of attitude did Martha serve?

Can you recall a time when you grumbled while serving? Explain.

Have you ever been resentful that others were not serving but you were?

Have you ever felt superior in any way because others were not serving but you were?

Did you ever feel exempt from serving?

What will happen if you get so busy serving that you neglect your relationship with God?

Was there ever a time that you became so busy that this happened to you?

What is the connection between worshipping and serving?

How does the story of what happened on the Mount of Transfiguration relate to this?

Chapter 4

The Attitude of a Servant

Under the inspiration of the Holy Spirit, the Apostle Paul begins the epistle to the Romans by saying, *"Paul, a bondservant of Jesus Christ."* What an introduction! Paul, a servant of love, *"of Jesus Christ, called to be an apostle, separated to the gospel of God"* (Romans 1:1).

What great concepts we find in this one verse alone—"bondservant," "called," "separated," "the gospel of God." In this verse we see both the attitude (that of a servant) and the anointing in ministry (the gifts and callings). Both are needed. The anointing or call of God is a grace gift, but the attitude is left to you to determine. Before God, you are a son, but before man, you see yourself in attitude as a bondservant.

Every anointed vessel must have the same attitude as Jesus: *"Let this mind* (or attitude) *be in you which was also in Christ Jesus"* (Philippians 2:5). What was His attitude? It was that of a humble servant.

You are given to a particular sphere of influence to be a servant to that sphere of influence; therefore, the anointing upon you is not for position or power but for you to be enabled by the Spirit of God to serve the community that God calls you to, whether it be a local church or an international ministry.

Paul was mighty in the Spirit. God used him in extraordinary ways, even to perform "unusual miracles." The dead were raised, the blind saw, the bound were delivered and healed, multitudes were touched, and churches were planted. In no way could Paul be called average. He was an anointed vessel whom God used to shape the Church of his generation, and even to this day, we are the beneficiaries of his ministry.

Paul saw himself as a servant.

Let us look once again at Romans 1:1—*"Paul, a bondservant of Jesus Christ, called to be an apostle, separated to the gospel of God."* Notice that despite being used mightily by God as an apostle, he calls himself a servant before an apostle. In the anointing, Paul was confident and secure in his calling as an apostle, but in attitude he was a bondservant.

Paul understood that the attitude of being a servant undergirded everything he did. There were times when he introduced himself as Paul, an apostle, called by God, but before his apostleship, he knew that he was a bondservant of God. While the attitude is the indispensable foundation of any calling, no one can successfully walk in an office or ministry gift without first walking in the attitude of a servant. Those who exalt their anointing and calling above the attitude of a servant will rise in pride and run the risk of damaging many lives, but those who walk in an attitude of humility are providing the right environment for their ministry anointing to flourish. Not only Paul, but Jesus Himself, had the attitude of a servant. The greatest of all, the Apostle of all apostles, the Leader of all leaders had the attitude of a servant.

Since all Christians have an anointing, gifting, and calling, this principle is applicable not just to the five-fold ministry but to every believer. Some Christians in the process of development are trying to discover the area of ministry in which they are gifted, but whatever this ministry turns out to be, it needs to be wrapped in the garment of a servant.

If we could live with this attitude that was in Jesus, we would doubtlessly have greater impact in our anointing and ministries. People will receive from us a whole lot more readily if they see that we are serving and caring, for it is the attitude that often speaks louder than the office or calling. Paul could raise the dead, cast out demons, and heal the sick, yet he did not walk in arrogance but in humility, because he had the attitude of Jesus. The key to anointed ministry is to make yourself a servant; only **then** will you have the right to exercise the gift in you with authority. Notice this attitude in Paul:

For though I am free from all men, ***I have made myself a servant to all,*** *that I might win the more.* (1 Corinthians 9:19)

Paul made himself a servant. How? In his attitude. Salvation made him a son and God called him to be an apostle, but Paul **made himself** in attitude a servant. It was this servant attitude that enabled him to impact and win people to Christ. This attitude in your life and calling will make your message attractive so that many will be touched by God through you.

Sometimes you will find that ministries can be very aloof, very rude, very uncaring. Every seed produces after its own kind, so an abusive or harsh leader or ministry will produce a harsh, critical, unloving, uncaring church or ministry. That is why the garment of servitude must be placed over your anointing.

There is no boasting about these callings, because they are not earned but given by God as He wills. If you want to fulfill your ministry, make sure that you are covered by the garment of a servant, not self-seeking but humble in attitude. Whether you are a preacher, teacher, children's worker, church planter, or are involved in any other area of ministry, the bottom line is that your purpose is to serve people. It should not come as a revelation that **you** are the ministry.

When Programs Take Precedence Over People

Pastors would do well to remember that ministry is people. Church programs, buildings, and finances are important, but something is seriously amiss when these things are allowed to take precedence over people. A pastor might be a great preacher with a large congregation, but he must first be a servant. The greater the calling of God, the greater the responsibility to be a servant. The flock will become like their pastor, developing into servants of God in their home, to their church, and then to the world.

Leaders will always have people who will serve their ministry. That is what we call sharing the vision. They serve these leaders because these leaders serve them; the followers connect to the leaders' vision and help them fulfill it. Understanding that every seed produces after its own kind, they know that one day they will have their own field, if they are faithful in another man's field. Thus, they join themselves not just to a ministry but to a vision, and they serve that vision.

You do not join a church because you find the pastor to be a good preacher and a friendly person; rather, you are, in fact, joining an anointing, a vision for your town, your region, and your nation. You do not just join a church, but you join a vision, and you choose to serve in that vision because the pastor serves you through his or her gifts. Thus, you serve that vision through yours and you become a team.

There is no place for hotshots or big names, because only one name counts, and that is the name above every name. We do not build ministries; we build His Church. We do not build a reputation; we lose it. We become co-laborers with Him. We become investors in His dream. His dream is the Church.

Leaders should serve people.

Not only was Paul mighty in God and humble in heart, but he knew that his ministry was not in position or title but in serving people. Much modern church leadership today lacks this quality. Some pastors and church leaders are far removed from the people, as if the people existed for the leaders rather than the other way around. Our gifts and callings are for the benefit of other people, so we serve them through these gifts and through our lives. Paul was even willing to be inconvenienced to the point of giving his life. He was willing to die. Hirelings do not give their lives but shepherds do. Hirelings will run when the pressure is on, but shepherds will fight to protect, to preserve, to keep.

In addition to Paul, other apostles also viewed themselves first and foremost as bondservants:

- *James, a bondservant of God and of the Lord Jesus Christ* (James 1:1)

- *Simon Peter, a bondservant and apostle of Jesus Christ* (2 Peter 1:1)

- *Jude, a bondservant of Jesus Christ, and brother of James* (Jude 1)

These great leaders of the early Church all made the choice to be bondservants in their attitude. Like them, we all need to make the decision to humble ourselves and take on the form of a bondservant. Much has been taught on gifting, anointing, and calling, but we should also be taught the need to have the right attitude—that of a servant. All these leaders were secure in their gifting, but they were equally secure in being seen in attitude as a servant.

Servants are scarce in today's Church, because we are living in a society that is self-seeking and self-absorbed. It is wicked, corrupt, and immoral, and that is why we must be an influence. As citizens of another Kingdom, we need to be salt and light. God's Kingdom is radically different from the selfish kingdom of this age. The Kingdom of God operates out of another spirit. We have not received the spirit of this world but we have received the Spirit who is from God (1 Corinthians 2:12), so we are under the influence of another spirit. The world is led by the lusts of the flesh and the eyes, being consumed by its own greed and selfishness. In contrast, we are led by the Spirit, by the Word, and by love, and we operate by faith. This Kingdom operates contrary to the world. The world is selfish, whereas we ought to be Christ-centered, seeking the welfare of others, and esteeming them above ourselves (Philippians 2:3).

Hypocrisy Among Christians

Many Christians live no differently than the world lives, but the world holds us to a higher standard. This standard is not required of any other religion but is required of the New Testament Church, because we insist that we alone have the answer—Jesus Christ. We claim that Jesus is the only way, and the world clamors to see the evidence of Him at work in our lives. They want to see that the Christian life is real, but, sadly, we are often rightfully called hypocrites and phonies, because we are living no differently than they are. Some need to repent, and some need to ask God for mercy and grace. Some leaders have acted in such a way that church leadership appears arrogant, proud, aloof, and untouchable. For a number of them, the people are actually an inconvenience, a mere means to an end rather than the goal and the fruit of ministry.

The Body of Christ needs changing, and this includes leaders. It does not matter if we call ourselves servants of God; what matters is whether **others** would call us servants. Why would they call us servants if they do not see us serving? Lorne Sanny, former president and general director of the Navigators, was quite astute when he remarked, "You find out what kind of servant you are by how you respond when you are treated like one."

God is at work in us to bring us to a place of servanthood, anointing, and character. He wants to raise up the Church to be Christ-centered, selfless, loving, giving, praying, faithful, diligent, and anointed. The anointing must be accompanied by excellence of character, because we are being conformed to the image of Jesus.

Jesus said, "Well done, good and faithful servant." We are not merely called to be servants but are expected to be good and faithful servants. In other words, God requires consistency in what we do. He commends good and faithful but rebukes lazy and wicked, requiring a higher standard of His people. He is calling us to be good, to be faithful, and to be servants in attitude. These diligent ones who go out of their way for the glory of God will prosper in all their efforts because He will expand their influence.

Epaphroditus went out of his way to serve Paul.

Passionate followers of Jesus will find themselves going out of their way to serve. One such person was Epaphroditus; though he is only mentioned briefly in Scripture (Philippians 2:25-30; 4:18), this exceptional man was the epitome of a true servant. Disregarding his own needs and well-being to selflessly give of his time and energy to Paul and the believers in Philippi, he was not a taker or consumer but served even to the point of risking his own life.

Yet I considered it necessary to send to you Epaphroditus, my brother, fellow worker, and fellow *soldier, but your messenger and the <u>one who ministered to my need</u>; since he was longing for you all, and was distressed because you had heard that he was sick. For indeed he was sick almost unto death; but God had mercy on him, and not only on him but on me also, lest I should have sorrow upon sorrow. Therefore I sent him the more eagerly, that when you see him again you may rejoice, and I may be less sorrowful. Receive him therefore in the Lord with all gladness, and hold such men in esteem; because for the work of Christ he came close to death, not regarding his life, to supply what was lacking in <u>your service</u> toward me.* (Philippians 2:25-30)

Notice Paul's description of Epaphroditus: "my brother," "fellow worker," "fellow soldier," and "your messenger."

My brother (relationship in the family of God): Some Christians are comfortable in the relationship of family but never proceed deeper into the relationship to become fellow workers. They enjoy fellowship, sharing in the Word, and church life but do not want to be "pressured" to step into action. Not so with this man of God; he was in relationship but also in ministry. Every Christian should become part of God's ministry team.

Fellow worker (relationship in the responsibility of sharing in the ministry): Epaphroditus was no lazy Christian sitting on the sidelines spectating and criticizing but was fully committed, jumping into the work of ministry to join forces with Paul and Timothy.

Too many Christians are happy to be in the family and to reap the benefits of Father's house yet feel no need for any involvement. The Greek word for "fellow worker" is "sunergos," from which we get the word "synergy," meaning "the working together of two things to produce an effect greater than the sum of their individual effects." The ministry of our local church will be enhanced when we become fellow workers. Instead of leaving all the work to a handful of faithful people, all believers ought to rise to the call of God and become fully employed in the work of ministry.

Fellow soldier (relationship in the advance of the gospel and the suffering endured to this end): Epaphroditus traveled a long distance from Philippi to carry the offering sent by the believers to Paul in Rome. Allowed to minister while under house arrest, Paul had a continuous stream of people visiting him even though he was still a prisoner and an enemy of Rome. Epaphroditus was willing to put himself at risk to go and work with Paul in the gospel and the growing of the local church. Ministry can be viewed as serving, but there is a battle as well. Circumstances will be against us, Satan and his cohorts will be against us, and at times even other believers may be against us. Ministry demands of us the heart of a servant and the will of a soldier.

Your messenger (relationship as a representative): In delivering the offering sent to help Paul, not only did Epaphroditus faithfully deliver it, but he also stayed to minister to (or serve) Paul. Going so far out of his way that he worked himself to the point of exhaustion and became sick, he was a genuine representative of the Lord and of the church in Philippi.

It is no coincidence that Paul writes about Epaphroditus in Philippians 2, the same chapter in which he addresses Jesus' abandoned life and attitude:

Let this mind be in you which was also in Christ Jesus, who, being in the form of God, did not consider it robbery to be equal with God, but made Himself of no reputation, taking the form of a bondservant, and coming in the likeness of men. (Philippians 2:5-7)

What an honor for Epaphroditus to be written about in the same context as the Lord. Truly this man had the same attitude as Jesus, but so can we. If we do, all of eternity will recall our abandoned, selfless lifestyle to the glory of God.

How far will you go?

The problem with many Christians is that they are content to remain in their comfort zone and do not want to be inconvenienced. On a ministry trip to Togo, West Africa, a man arrived at my meeting at eleven o'clock at night. Confined to a wheelchair and having no legs, he had left his home early that morning to wheel himself more than seven miles over dirt roads for the sole purpose of receiving prayer. After prayer, he was going to push himself all the way back home again, but we made sure that he was accommodated and that someone would take him back the next day. We prayed for him, but I was so impressed by his passion that caused him to go so far out of his way for God.

I had also gone out of my way to be there, traveling about thirty hours, mostly in uncomfortable, crowded, hot airplanes in which it was so tight that I could not even eat my food or get any sleep. Traveling an additional seven hours to get to the village, my team and I preached from sunrise to 11 o'clock at night. I went out of my way to serve God.

Some believers just want a Christianity of convenience. Their question is not, "What can I do for God?" but "What can God do for me?" They want heaven, blessing, prosperity, and health, but they do not want to be "inconvenienced" by doing something for God. They want to be called servants of God because they like the title, but they do not want to serve. They want the power and the anointing but do not want to go out of their way. If they do serve but are inconvenienced, they will let you know it (often, by not showing up), but servants will serve even when inconvenienced.

Will you serve when it is uncomfortable? Will you serve when you are busy? How far out of your way will you go for God? Will you go as far as that man in the wheelchair? Too many Christians today are comfort-zone, namby-pamby, gutless, weak-kneed wimps, but God is looking for faithful, diligent servants, people who will get busy for Him. When God called Moses, he was tending his father-in-law's sheep. When God called Elisha, he was plowing his father's field. When God called David, he was taking care of his father's sheep. When God called Joshua, he was serving Moses. When God called Nehemiah, he was the king's cupbearer, a servant.

God calls busy people.

God calls busy people, not the lazy. He calls good and faithful people to anointed living. The fishermen were busy, Matthew was busy, Jesus was busy. If we are going to reach a generation of hardened sinners, impact this world and see the Church grow and be restored to Pentecostal power, it will begin with our being servants and carrying out God's business.

We will be required to be faithful and diligent in all the business of the Kingdom. Though some people despise this four-letter word, "work," it has been said that the ministry is spelled "w-o-r-k." There is simply no place in this holy Kingdom to be slothful and apathetic.

I am a preacher of grace; I believe that our best works could never secure our salvation, for they would be like dirty rags. Being saved by grace through faith, our only boast is in the Cross. While we are not saved **by** works (Ephesians 2:8-9), we are saved **for** good works (Ephesians 2:10). In fact, Paul says that God's people are zealous for good works (Titus 2:14), meaning that they are passionately engaged in those works. The grace of God that saves us is the same grace that empowers us to be servants, zealously occupied in the work of ministry.

Another Believer who went out of his way to Serve

The Lord grant mercy to the household of Onesiphorus, for he often refreshed me, and was not ashamed of my chain; but when he arrived in Rome, he sought me out very zealously and found me. The Lord grant to him that he may find mercy from the Lord in that Day—and you know very well how many ways he ministered to me at Ephesus. (2 Timothy 1:16-18)

Onesiphorus went against the tide of public opinion, doing what others were not willing to do. In the context of the above passage, people were turning away from Paul, probably because of the risk to their own well-being or because they had been persuaded away from the faith. Nevertheless, while everyone was deserting him, Onesiphorus went out of his way to serve Paul. As an honest-to-goodness profitable servant, he was aptly named: "Onesiphorus" means "profit-bearing."

It appears that today's Christians are fickle and will hunt with the hounds or run with the foxes. They are not willing to actually go out of their way to serve the local church and the people to whom God connects them. We need people just like Onesiphorus who will rise to the call of God to be servants instead of waiting to be served. Will you dare to swim upstream? Listen, even dead fish can float downstream. I challenge you to become like Onesiphorus (you can keep your own name!) and be mentioned in the annals of eternity because you became a servant. You can invest your life into something that will speak forever about your love for God.

How far is far enough?

In this book I am stirring you for service, challenging you to be committed "second-milers" who will go way out of your way to serve God. I am encouraging you to live sacrificially and to be willing to suffer for the sake of the Kingdom. Having said that, I must confess that I have seen well-meaning, devoted Christians who have suffered abuse by being worked to the place of exhaustion or offense.

On the one hand, I say, "Go way out of your way to serve God." But on the other hand, I am going to say, "Watch out that you do not get used and abused in the name of being a servant." I have seen people serve and serve and serve to the point of getting burned out. This is the natural result when the responsibility of ministry falls solely on the dedicated core of about 10% to 20% of the local church.

The 80% who do nothing will remain inactive, because no demand is ever placed on them to change. Some leaders become so dependent on the loyal handful that every job gets delegated to them. Eventually these people who do everything become burned out and in the process, find themselves neglecting their home, family, and business. There ought to be a point where the workload is spread out. While every believer should do his or her part, it must not be to the point of abuse or neglecting the home. Lamentably, some neglect their homes, spouses, and families, all in the name of being a servant.

My advice to the Onesiphorus type of Christian is to serve faithfully and sacrificially but to recognize that you cannot do it all. You must also rest and make time for family and for yourself. Do not get "guilted" into serving, but follow your heart and learn when to say, "That's far enough." See to it that the ones delegating work to you raise up others to serve in addition to you. Other believers must step up to the plate and take their place in the ranks of serving in the church. Do not aid and abet the slackness of others by your diligence.

My advice to pastors and leaders who are delegating tasks is to ensure that you do not saddle your most-loyal people with everything while others remain idle. Go to the complacent, challenging them to become involved and devoted to a lifestyle of service.

Ministry is Serving

And I thank Christ Jesus our Lord who has enabled me, because He counted me faithful, putting me into the ministry. (1 Timothy 1:12)

Ministry is generally seen as preaching, praying, and prophesying, but in reality it is serving. The word "ministry" in the verse above is the word from which we get the word "deacon," so we see that Paul was placed into the ministry, i.e., the role of a servant, an attendant or an aide. Finding him faithful, God called him into servanthood. He puts faithful people whom He enables into the ministry. How does He enable us? By the anointing. He supplies the grace and the anointing, but it is up to us to possess the attitude of a servant.

Simply defined, ministry is serving; that is what the word "ministry" means. God puts faithful believers into the ministry, giving them a Bible in one hand and a toilet brush (signifying service) in the other. In essence, He is saying, "Look, I am giving you power but I am also giving you things that have to be done, because there will be messy situations that you will need to clean up; if you cannot clean a toilet, most probably you will never be faithful to clean up people's lives."

Ministry is doing **what** needs to be done **when** it needs to be done. Until you get that revelation, you are always aspiring to ministry, but ministry is really just doing what needs to be done at any given point, whether it is viewed as practical or viewed as spiritual.

Ministry is developed on your knees with a toilet brush in your hand, not just on your knees praying. When you can serve in the practical and do what others do not want to do, God will trust you with people. That is the place where ministry is formed.

Everyone should be trained in the Word and in the operations of the Spirit, but those things based on anointing without the right attitude are dangerous. Often, emerging preachers go straight from Bible school into a pulpit, and though they are well-trained theologically, they have not been trained to serve. They expect the people to serve them and their vision but they themselves have not served the people. Many Bible schools are producing theologians but not servant leaders, thus engendering a lukewarm church of selfish people. Perhaps the followers have become just like their leaders.

Jesus made the disciples servants, because at the end of His ministry He said, *"No longer do I call you servants...but I have called you friends"* (John 15:15). In other words, "I am taking our relationship to a new level, a level of increase, a place of promotion; you will always be servants in heart and attitude but I call you friends." He discipled (taught and trained) them by first making them servants; later they would become caring and diligent servant leaders. Every believer is a minister and should therefore be released into his ministry role through serving.

We have seen that the anointing and the attitude must work hand in hand, but the way to increase in the anointing is through serving. Freely you have received, freely give. If you do not give away what you have gotten, you will never get more. The anointing does not grow in the idle but rather in faithful servants.

All of us should have the willingness to carry the bowl and towel in addition to the willingness to carry the Bible. We must assume the responsibility to help those in need, being quick to wash the feet of those who could use an act of kindness.

Our Relationship to God

In our walk with God and in our approach to God, we are always sons and daughters, but in our ministry on earth, we represent Him as servants. I approach Father God not as a servant but a son, but I approach humanity the way Jesus did—as a servant. Jesus not only served but was a servant.

Fulfill my joy by being like-minded, having the same love, being of one accord, of one mind. Let nothing be done through selfish ambition or conceit, but in lowliness of mind let each esteem others better than himself. Let each of you look out not only for his own interests, but also for the interests of others. (Philippians 2:2-4)

If you are going to do something, do not do it with the motive of selfish ambition or conceit.

...but in lowliness of mind (v. 2)

The attitude of a servant is humility. Attitudes are quite visible. For example, have you ever had a waitress in a restaurant that had a bad attitude even though you did nothing to cause it? Attitudes are very powerful, whether negative or positive. Jesus had an attitude, but His was one of humility because He was a servant.

...let each esteem others better than himself. Let each of you look out not only for his own interests, but also for the interests of others. (vv. 3-4)

Kingdom ministry is looking out for the interests of others. Kingdom ministry is humility of mind. Kingdom ministry is esteeming others better than yourself. The world is motivated by selfish ambition, conceit, egotism, self-interest. Kingdom ministry and leadership operate on a much loftier plane: from the position of the bowl and towel. We are citizens of that glorious Kingdom.

Your attitude should be the same as that of Christ Jesus. (Philippians 2:5 NIV)

His attitude was that of a servant. He was a Son, legitimately, but He made Himself of no reputation, taking on the form of a bondservant and becoming obedient even to the point of death. God exalted Him because of His obedience, humility, servanthood, giving, and sacrificial living. The way to increase in God is to humble yourself and become a servant.

You can cooperate by yielding, or you can resist what the Spirit of God wants to do. He is pouring out His Spirit to make you a servant, but in order to be made, you have to surrender to Him. When we sing, "Lord, make me like You," we are actually saying, "God, our attitude is to be like yours." He says, "If you will yield to Me, I will make you, but if you resist Me there is nothing I can do about it because this is your decision."

No Pressure in the Kingdom

Because of grace you do not have to do anything, but because of grace you **want** to do everything that is pure and holy and good. You are not trying to obtain something; you already have it, and because you have it, you do it. This is the Kingdom.

A bondservant is a slave who chooses the way of servitude. Despite the fact that he is redeemed and allowed to go free, he submits himself to the doorpost to have his ear pierced with an awl, thus proclaiming for all his life, "I am a servant of my master."

Now these are the judgments which you shall set before them: If you buy a Hebrew servant, he shall serve six years; and in the seventh he shall go out free and pay nothing. If he comes in by himself, he shall go out by himself; if he comes in married, then his wife shall go out with him. If his master has given him a wife, and she has borne him sons or daughters, the wife and her children shall be her master's, and he shall go out by himself. But if the servant plainly says, 'I love my master, my wife, and my children; I will not go out free,' then his master shall bring him to the judges. He shall also bring him to the door, or to the doorpost, and his master shall pierce his ear with an awl; and he shall serve him forever. (Exodus 21:1-6)

Jesus came as a servant, making Himself of no reputation. He was marked at the tree, forever to be seen and marked as a servant. We choose the way of a servant, also going to the cross and having our ear pierced to be marked with the mark of a servant, that God has our ear. We give our life to Him; He does not take it, but we freely **give** it.

In summary:

- Our attitude as servants speaks louder than our title or position.

- Our position as servants is more visible than our gifts, ministries, and callings.

- True greatness is being like Jesus. We can serve but not be servants in attitude. When we are servants in attitude, we are truly followers of Jesus, and this is the measure of greatness.

- The problem with many Christians is that they are content in their comfort zone and do not want to be inconvenienced. Passion will always take us out of our way.

> **Questions:**
>
> Do you consider "ministry" as something that you are not involved in yet but that you aspire to? If so, how will you know when you have "entered" ministry?
>
>
> How would you define ministry? Do you see people as the goal of ministry or as a means to an end?
>
>
> When you think of ministry, do you connect it with serving?
>
>
> Have you ever served grudgingly?

Have you felt like you were doing someone a big favor when you served?

Paul, Peter, James, and Jude called themselves bondservants. Do you see yourself as one? Explain.

How did Epaphroditus and Onesiphorus serve Paul?

Among other things, Paul called Epaphroditus his brother and fellow worker. Are you a brother only or are you also a fellow worker?

Why must the garment of a servant be placed over your gift and calling?

When the unsaved look at your life, do they see a servant? Would they have evidence that you are one?

How do you feel about going out of your way to serve someone?

Have you ever served in a certain capacity in church but then you gave it up? Why?

Can you think of an instance when you were inconvenienced? How did you feel about it?

Can you think of an instance when someone else went out of his or her way for you?

The Attitude of a Servant

Are you a comfort-zone Christian or do you go out of your way to help others?

Are you a servant in attitude?

Chapter 5

The Anointing of a Servant

*"In the Last Days," God says, "I will pour out my Spirit on every kind of people: Your sons will prophesy, also your daughters; your young men will see visions, your old men dream dreams. When the time comes, **I'll pour out my Spirit on those who serve me, men and women both**, and they'll prophesy."* (Acts 2:17-18 Message Bible)

The purpose of Pentecost goes beyond the ability to speak in tongues; the Holy Spirit has also provided us with the power to be witnesses and to be a people of visions and dreams. But over and above all these things, God has poured out His Spirit so that those who are touched and empowered will become servants operating in the earth with the spirit of Jesus. Thus, the actual purpose of the outpouring of God's Spirit is not just to empower all flesh but specifically menservants and maidservants. The Holy Spirit is not given to people who just want to feel God but to those who will take responsibility and stewardship. This involves stewardship not just of their finances but of their lives, time, vision, and ministry. God is moving in the earth today to raise up the Church to serve Him.

"Even on my servants, both men and women, I will pour out my Spirit in those days" (Acts 2:18 NIV).

This day, God is pouring out His Spirit upon servant-hearted people.

Why God is Pouring out His Spirit on Servants

Since many Christians are too busy with their own priorities to make time for God's purposes, He specifically pours out His Spirit on servant-hearted people, because they will carry the mandate. They are broken, humble, yielded, and surrendered, having abdicated the throne of their will to make Jesus the Lord of their lives. Because their satisfaction derives from pleasing Him, they are willing to take upon themselves the responsibility for making His business their business.

The Spirit of God is not seeking out people who only want to be touched, but those willing to be touched, changed, and empowered to serve. The former do not care about the nations, the lost, the hungry and the naked because they are selfish, self-willed, self-driven, and self-made. That is why God is deliberately looking for servant-hearted people; He knows that they are the ones who will gladly yield their lives to fulfill His will in the earth.

Servant-hearted people have come out of slavery to sin and have now been embraced by the grace of God. Putting great value to what He has done for them, they no longer serve themselves but serve Him. These are the ones who are going to be carriers of the power of

God. He is pouring out His Spirit on all flesh, but in a greater way on a serving people who are pouring out of themselves.

That is why Jesus said, *"He who believes in Me, as the Scripture has said, out of his heart will flow rivers of living water"* (John 7:38). What gets into you flows out of you. When you get into the river of God, that river gets into you and changes you to become conformed to the image of Christ, the servant. You, thus, become part of a serving and sacrificial people who willingly pour out that which has been poured into them. That is what it means to be touched by God and empowered to serve.

The people in the room and the city were impacted.

God's Spirit fell mightily in the upper room: sound came from heaven like a mighty rushing wind and tongues of fire appeared upon each one. All were filled with the Spirit as God's glory filled the house. His presence was so intense that they began to exalt God by speaking in other tongues.

The impact of this event was felt throughout the entire city as multitudes came rushing to see what was happening. In the aftermath, Peter stood up to preach, starting his message by quoting the prophet Joel.

"And it shall come to pass in the last days, says God, that I will pour out of My Spirit on all flesh; your sons and your daughters shall prophesy, your young men shall see visions, your old men shall dream dreams, and

on My menservants and on My maidservants I will pour out My Spirit in those days."* (Acts 2:17-18)

We are recipients of the outpouring of the Spirit that is moving throughout the whole earth. God is looking for a people to become carriers of His name and His power who will represent Him, not just as His sons and daughters, but as those who will represent Him as servants of God.

God is not pouring out His Spirit just so that we can have great meetings. Though I love great meetings, I want something greater than meetings—I want to see lives changed and impacted to the point of action. All too often lives are touched, but it does not lead to action. We see the principle of being touched by God and empowered to serve in the account of Jesus ministering to Peter's mother-in-law.

Now as soon as they had come out of the synagogue, they entered the house of Simon and Andrew, with James and John. But Simon's wife's mother lay sick with a fever, and they told Him about her at once. So He came and took her by the hand and lifted her up, and immediately the fever left her. **And she served them.** (Mark 1:29-31)

Jesus heals Peter's mother-in-law.

Because she was immobilized, Peter's mother-in-law was not able to serve. You cannot serve when you are immobilized. But when Jesus steps onto the scene, your life and circumstances are about to change. When Jesus walked into that room, He touched her and something happened—the fever left and she was made whole. As a result of His touch, she now served them. Just as she served them as a result of His touch, we should also rise up to serve others as a result of His touch upon our lives.

It is significant that He takes her by the hand, because the hand represents service. He takes her hand because He not only wants to touch her body but release her into her destiny. He touches her, eliminates the problem that is restricting her movement, and then with the hand that was touched, she serves them. She serves **them**—Jesus **and** those with Him. Too many Christians want to serve the Lord but not His people; they do not mind serving God but do not really have time for the people. She served Jesus and those who were with Him, because when we touch them, we touch Him. When we do it to them, we do it to Him. When we bring a glass of water to one of them—to even the least of them—we do it to Him. When we neglect them, we neglect Him.

You cannot be touched by the nail-scarred hand of Jesus and be the same. When He touches you, you want to do something. After being healed by Jesus, Peter's mother-in-law served them. Why? She did it because Jesus was there and others were there, and they were hungry. When you serve others, you serve Him. When you serve Him, you serve others. What you do in His name to someone else, you do to Him. And so you are not just serving somebody or other; you are actually serving Jesus. He touches you to raise you up, removing the limits that are upon your life so that you can serve both Him and them.

In our Western worldview, we have wrongly divided the spiritual and the practical, the sacred and the secular. We do not see ourselves as spiritual beings and that everything we do is, therefore, spiritual. But when you feed, care, and help practically, as in the washing of the feet, it does not have to be a spiritual "church thing." It could be buying a big bucket of paint and painting the home of a person who cannot afford to have it painted. It could be picking up an elderly man's car to take it for an oil change. It could be cleaning a woman's home while she is struggling in her health. All of these things are practical, yet they are also spiritual because what you do to them is also being done to Him. When we serve them, we serve Him.

Servants are fruitful.

There is something about the Kingdom—there must be fruit. Jesus tells us to abide in Him, the true vine, so that we may bear much fruit. If we bear fruit, the Father will prune us so that we may bear even more fruit. Thus, we see that we can have some fruit, we can have more fruit, and we can have much fruit. Much fruit glorifies God. We bring Him glory by representing Him well as servants. The outpouring of the Spirit is to change us so that we can become servants of God.

Not everyone will stand at a podium to preach or go to a foreign land and take a village or a nation, but everyone can serve God. It is not only missionaries and pastors who are spiritual; we are **all** spiritual. Whether serving in greeting, cleaning, maintenance, sound, worship or the nursery, it is all spiritual and will have an eternal result.

If you are working in the kitchen serving meals or in the nursery caring for babies, do not think that these areas are not spiritual. Everything you do is spiritual. It is a total misconception to believe that you are not spiritual unless you are a preacher or part of the worship team. Whether you go to work in the morning or stay home and look after the children, it is spiritual.

God empowers us not just to preach, cast out demons, and heal the sick, but also to serve at tables, to help those in need, to lift the bruised and the broken, and to care for orphans. It takes an anointing to work with children, be a helper in the meetings, or be a good sound technician. Every Christian should be a vehicle for the glory of God.

Some things are considered mundane or practical rather than spiritual, but we should rely on God even in these ordinary tasks. Our skills, experience, and knowledge may not be enough. We need God's ability and grace for those specific areas of ministry that He has called us into.

Waiting on tables was entrusted to Spirit-filled believers.

When the apostles found that the pressure of all the work caused some people to be neglected, they appointed what have been called "deacons" to assist them. In order to be selected, candidates would have to be Spirit-filled, thus demonstrating that the anointing of God is necessary not only for miracles (as vital and spiritual as these are) but just as much to care and to serve. This is a biblical example of the practical and the spiritual being one and the same. These were people who were as comfortable operating in the supernatural as they were in the natural. Caring and serving are every bit as spiritual as preaching and teaching.

Then the twelve summoned the multitude of the disciples and said, "It is not desirable that we should leave the word of God and serve tables. Therefore, brethren, seek out from among you seven men of good reputation, **full of the Holy Spirit** *and wisdom, whom we may appoint over this business.* (Acts 6:2-3)

Stretch out your hand.

Now it happened on another Sabbath, also, that He entered the synagogue and taught. And a man was there whose right hand was withered. So the scribes and Pharisees watched Him closely, whether He would heal on the Sabbath, that they might find an accusation against Him. But he knew their thoughts, and said to the man who had the withered hand, "Arise and stand here." And he arose and stood. Then Jesus said to them, "I will ask you one thing: Is it lawful on the Sabbath to do good or to do evil, to save life or to destroy?" And when He had looked around at them all, He said to the man, "Stretch out your hand." And he did so, and his hand was restored as whole as the other. But they were filled with rage, and discussed with one another what they might do to Jesus. (Luke 6:6-11)

The scribes and Pharisees believed that Jesus would be breaking the law if He were to heal on the Sabbath, but doing good does not break the law. It is because of the grace of God that we do good works, not in order to obtain salvation, but because we **already** have it. We engage in operations of faith because we **are** at rest, not to gain our rest.

Many Christians have a withered right hand. It has learned how to pray, to worship, and even to receive, but it is not serving God. We have churches with withered hands. We have been restored in worship, in prayer, and even in giving, but have we been restored to serve? I say we are in the process. One hand is fine but the other hand needs healing. Just as Jesus touched Peter's mother-in-law's hand and she rose to serve, so I believe Jesus is touching our withered hand so that every Christian becomes a servant.

It would be very difficult for a defective part of your body to function at full potential. Today, the Body of Christ is not functioning at full potential because of missing, deformed or dysfunctional parts. There are many joints that are not connected and other parts whose gifts and callings have been ignored, but God wants every Christian a minister, every Christian a servant.

It is time to arise.

Just as with the man with the withered hand in the synagogue, God is saying to you, "Arise and stand here." He is calling you to attention to get ready for what He is about to do. We must take responsibility for our wholeness and our healing by arising and going to where Jesus is found working. Let us get to the place where He can touch us. Way too many are sitting down with a withered hand when they should be standing up. He says to you today, "Arise and stand here, because I am about to do something for you; I am going to remove the hindrances that keep you from fulfilling your maximum potential."

In the above portion of Scripture, Jesus did not pull up the man and make him whole; the **man** with the withered hand arose and stood up by himself, showing that he had to cooperate with God. It is not just what God will do but it is what **we** will do.

Revival comes and God begins to pour out His Spirit, but will we embrace it? God will do it, but will we stand up and get in line for what He wants to do? Many will acknowledge that God is moving, but not many will stand up to be a part of what He is doing. He is calling us to attention because He wants our right hand to be restored. The right hand is known as the hand of power, and it is the hand that carries the bowl and towel because that is the hand of Jesus. This hand is so powerful that it can cast out demons and heal the sick, yet it can also wash dirty feet. In other words, it is ready to do whatever needs doing at any given moment.

The man's withered hand was healed on the Sabbath, and I believe that we New Testament Christians are living in our Sabbath rest. Jesus finished the work required for redemption once and for all through His substitutionary death upon the Cross.

We can do nothing to earn our salvation. When I talk about service and works and sacrifice, it is not to **add** to the Cross but rather is the **result** of the Cross. He has done it all. There is nothing that we can contribute to the finished work of the Cross other than to put our trust in Him and what He has done for us. The work is complete; it is forever finished.

Saved by Grace

We are the recipients of the grace of God, saved through faith and not works. Works cannot save us or make us spiritual. It is the work of God within us that makes us spiritual, and we merely respond in obedience. We are in our rest, and there is nothing that we need to do to earn entrance into heaven; the way has already been made for us by the precious blood of Jesus that has cleansed us from all guilt and sin. As we appropriate by faith the provision of the substitutionary death of Christ, we are saved from our sins **and** set apart for the work of God. The blood saves us and makes us vessels for His holy service.

As we become active in serving God, we need to remember that just as we do not do works to get saved, we also do not do works in order to stay saved. We neither get saved nor "maintain" our salvation through works. Christians who do not engage in works will not lose their salvation but will miss out on rewards. We are involved and committed to the work of God not in order to be saved or to stay saved but because we **are** saved. Some erroneously believe that since we are saved apart from works, there is no need to do anything for God. However, the grace that saves us also empowers us to be full participants in the works of ministry.

We are released and we are free, but our freedom is to serve, to love, and to build. Our freedom is not to become lazy. Though we cannot get right with God through our works, *"we are His workmanship, created in Christ Jesus for good works"* (Ephesians 2:10). If salvation were based on works, we would have to work a whole lot harder because even our best works would be considered as filthy rags. We could never attain the measure because the measure had to be perfection and none but Christ could reach it.

I am a preacher of grace. We deserved hell, but the grace of God has saved us through faith and plucked us out of hell's flames. Despite the fact that we were all citizens of the kingdom of darkness, God's love came to us and rescued us and brought us out. It is most unfortunate that in many churches, grace is taught in such a way as to dangerously minimize the importance of works.

There is good work that is waiting be done, not the work of self-effort, but the work of the Spirit through yielded vessels. It is not being driven in a feeble attempt to be found acceptable, but being led by the Spirit. It is not working in order to **obtain** salvation, but rather as the **result** of the gift of salvation that we have freely received. It can be summarized in the motto of the Salvation Army, "Saved to Serve." We are saved not just to sit back until Jesus comes but we are saved to serve.

Blood and Fire

In the center of the Salvation Army flag are the words, "Blood and Fire." The blood redeems us and the fire empowers us. We are saved by the blood, but the fire ignites us to serve. The blood separates us, sanctifies us, purifies us, and gives us position and standing, but the fire gives us zeal, passion, vision, and releases us into the works that have been prepared for us to do.

Just as Jesus came at an appointed time, we are at our appointed time. There is a day for you and me to fulfill our role in heaven's plan, and we do that by giving our lives over to the service of God. Though we have entered into our Sabbath rest, we **want** to do everything because He has done everything. Because He has given **His** all, our response is, "I want to give **my** all." It is not about how much we can hold back but about how much we can give, not about what we can get **out** of this but what we can give **into** this! Selfishness says, "I don't have to do anything" and "What can I get out of this?" Sacrifice says, "What can I put into this?" not because I have to, but because I want to, I choose to. While our salvation is by grace through faith and not by our performance, it is wrong to believe that grace means that we do nothing; rather, it means that we are not bound by law to perform but are bound by love to serve.

Be ablaze with the Spirit.

We are told not to lag in diligence but to be fervent in spirit, serving the Lord (Romans 12:11). One translation says, *"Don't burn out; keep yourselves fueled and aflame. Be alert servants of the Master"* (Message Bible).

It is because of Pentecostal power that we can serve God. It is because of the work of the Spirit that we are empowered to serve. The reason many Christians are lagging in diligence is that they are not fueled by the Spirit. We have always thought that it was apathy that stopped people from serving God, but it is more than that—it is a lack of fire.

But now we have been delivered from the law, having died to what we were held by, so that we should serve in the newness of the Spirit and not in the oldness of the letter. (Romans 7:6)

Love makes you a servant, grace makes you a servant, the Spirit makes you a servant. The law cannot make you a servant but only a victim of judgment, because your works will never save you. Stretch forth your hand. God wants to raise you up.

In summary:

- God pours out His Spirit on servant-hearted people because He knows that they will rise to the occasion and carry the anointing to this generation.

- There is nothing wrong with wanting to be touched by God, because He desires to reach out and touch His children. However, those who have been touched by Him become carriers of His power and anointing and thus need to touch the lives of others.

- Too many Christians are in the ministry line but are not ministers. It is fine to receive ministry through the laying on of hands, but something is amiss if you are perpetually a recipient; God expects that at some point you will become a giver of what you receive.

- Just as Peter's mother-in-in-law was touched by Jesus and immediately began to serve, we too have received His outstretched hand upon our lives and should rise to serve someone else.

Questions:

What does the world consider greatness? How is greatness defined by the world?

What does Jesus consider greatness? How is greatness defined in the Kingdom of God?

Do you desire to be great? What do you mean by great? How do you plan to attain it?

Did you ever believe that you had to do works to keep your salvation?

How does the world view servants?

On whom does God pour out His Spirit? Why does He choose those people?

What was the purpose of the outpouring of God's Spirit?

What did Peter's mother-in-law do after Jesus healed her?

Have you ever felt that you wanted to serve God but not serve people?

Would washing someone else's car be considered spiritual or practical? Explain.

Are you part of the ministry team or are you the one standing in line waiting to be ministered to?

Chapter 6

The Motive of a Servant

For David, after he had served his own generation by the will of God, fell asleep, was buried with his fathers, and saw corruption. (Acts 13:36)

David served his generation because he was a man after the heart of God. Taking responsibility for God's entrustment, he did what was required of him. Like David, those with a heart after God are motivated by faith, love, and passion.

"Motive" is defined as "something (as a need or desire) that causes a person to act; that which incites to action."

At a huge church in South Africa, the parking lot attendant was a multi-millionaire. Despite being offered various "high-powered" positions in the church, he was happy with his white coat and his little flashlight to get the cars into the lot. At his day job, he would sit in a big office and make decisions that affected entire nations, but when he went to church, he found his pleasure in being the parking attendant. Now **that** is a secure person. He would smile and wave the cars in because he loved what he was doing. He did not consider it too menial a task; it was what he wanted to do to please God as well as what God had called him to do. He was being just like Jesus, who had all the position and title that anyone could ever have, but laid these down to serve.

With a Toilet Brush in one Hand

A friend of mine who went on to become a renowned pastor with one of the largest churches in Soweto told the story of how his ministry was birthed cleaning toilets. At first he felt humiliated because he had come from an educated and prominent family, but when he got his heart right, God promoted him and gave him one of the largest churches in the nation.

A servant does not serve for promotion, title or recognition. He is not motivated by fear or guilt but simply by the desire to please God. He is a servant, therefore, he serves. What you are, you do.

Negative motives such as envy, strife, and selfish ambition come straight out of the kingdom of darkness. People will act either out of the motive of selfish ambition or the motive of love. Those who are sincere and act out of goodwill are motivated by love.

A servant is genuine to the core, having no ulterior motives. He has nothing to prove and nothing to lose. His life is laid bare before God. He is not trying to gain acceptance or approval; he has it. You have it. You are accepted in the beloved, already approved by God. It is an action of genuine care that is prompted by the love of God that is in your heart and by your desire to do what pleases Him. A servant is secure in his identity and is, therefore, not intimidated by the lowliness of the task.

During a time that Smith Wigglesworth had gotten so busy with his plumbing business that his fire for God had waned, he got so upset with his wife one night that he locked her out of the house. When he unlocked the door in the morning to let her in after an entire night on the porch, she acted as if nothing had happened and proceeded to make him his favorite breakfast. It was her noble and selfless attitude that brought him back to the Lord. Servanthood is very powerful. Saved or unsaved, serve your family whether or not they respond to you in the way you think you deserve. Lay aside all pettiness and just do the right thing because it needs to be done.

How do true, godly servants carry out their tasks?

> ➤ **They serve with joy.**

Serve the LORD with gladness; come before His presence with singing. (Psalm 100:2)

Because you did not serve the LORD your God with joy and gladness of heart, for the abundance of everything, therefore you shall serve your enemies, whom the LORD will send against you, in hunger, in thirst, in nakedness, and in need of everything; and He will put a yoke of iron on your neck until He has destroyed you. (Deuteronomy 28:47-48)

As believers, it is essential that we represent God with zeal. However, this zeal should not make us miserable and driven, because it is in our joy that we best reveal God's presence. In both of these passages, we are told to serve the Lord with gladness, not with madness or a bad attitude. It is always a pleasure and a delight to serve Him. God does not place a burden upon us when He calls us to represent Him; His yoke is light and easy to wear, because He gives us joy in service. This joy is our strength. Since He is not served by human hands as though He needed anything (Acts 17:25), serving is not our gift to God but His gift to us. It is because of His love for us that He grants us the honor of co-laboring with Him to express that love joyfully to all mankind.

> ➢ **They serve with sincerity of heart.**

Bondservants, obey in all things your masters according to the flesh, not with eyeservice, as men-pleasers, but in **sincerity of heart***, fearing God. And whatever you do, do it heartily, as to the Lord and not to men, knowing that from the Lord you will receive the reward of the inheritance; for you serve the Lord Christ. But he who does wrong will be repaid for what he has done, and there is no partiality.* (Colossians 3:22-25)

"Haplotes," the Greek word for "sincerity," is defined as "singleness, simplicity, generosity, bountifulness, without dissimulation or self-seeking."

The Message Bible conveys this principle more clearly. Bear in mind that Paul was addressing real slaves, some of whom may have been working for masters who were abusive and harsh with them. Nevertheless, the wise apostle encourages them to do their best as unto the Lord.

Servants, do what you're told by your earthly masters. And don't just do the minimum that will get you by. ***Do your best****. Work from the heart for your real Master, for God, confident that you'll get paid in full when you come into your inheritance. Keep in mind always that the ultimate Master you're serving is Christ. The sullen servant who does shoddy work will be held responsible. Being Christian doesn't cover up bad work.* (Colossians 3:22-25 Message Bible)

To serve with sincerity of heart is to serve liberally or bountifully. We do not do it because we are pressured to perform but because our heart is sincere. We know that what we are doing is an investment of what Christ has invested in us. We become an extension of His love. We place value on Jesus and what is important to Him, making His priorities our priorities. Thus, our service is not a performance but springs naturally from the overflow of a pure heart.

➢ **They serve with love.**

***Christ's love has moved me to such extremes. His love** has the first and last word in everything we do. Our firm* *decision is to work from **this focused center**: One man died for everyone. That puts everyone in the same boat.* (2 Corinthians 5:13-14 Message Bible)

It is absolutely clear that God has called you to a free life. Just make sure that you don't use this freedom as an excuse to do whatever you want to do and destroy your freedom. Rather, use your freedom to serve one another in love; that's how freedom grows. (Galatians 5:13 Message Bible)

Without love, whatever we do has no lasting value. Love is the most powerful and attractive force in the universe, for God is love and everyone born of God walks in His love. It is the love for God and the love from God that propels us forth into acts of kindness and service. This love is not in word only but is always expressed in action.

> ➤ **They serve with zeal.**

Zeal can be defined as "eagerness and ardent interest in pursuit of something."

*And now, Israel, what does the LORD your God require of you, but to fear the LORD your God, to walk in all His ways and to love Him, to **serve the LORD your God with all your heart and with all your soul**.* (Deuteronomy 10:12)

*...not lagging in diligence, **fervent in spirit**, serving the Lord.* (Romans 12:11)

*...who gave Himself for us, that He might redeem us from every lawless deed and purify for Himself His own special people, **zealous for good works**.* (Titus 2:14)

We should be excited and passionate about the work of God, because His redemption has granted us everlasting access to His Throne. Jesus Himself was moved zealously when he went into the Temple of God—it was zeal for his Father's house that caused Him to be so radical. This society that is so extreme in its passion for the things of the world will never be impressed with the gospel nor be drawn to Jesus if we are halfhearted, casual, or indifferent. If we are not radical in our zeal for God, we will never impact or win them. Our passion and enthusiasm will demonstrate our love for God and draw them to the importance and attractiveness of what we believe.

> ➢ **They serve with humility.**

Serving the Lord with all humility, *with many tears and trials which happened to me by the plotting of the Jews.* (Acts 20:19)

Here is Andrew Murray's description of humility:

"Humility is perfect quietness of heart. It is for me to have no trouble; never to be fretted or vexed or irritated or sore or disappointed. It is to expect nothing, to wonder at nothing that is done to me, to feel nothing done against me. It is to be at rest when nobody praises me, and when I am blamed or despised. It is to have a blessed home in the Lord, where I can go in and shut the door, and kneel to my Father in secret, and am at peace as in a deep sea of calmness, when all around and above is trouble."

In our passionate pursuit to make Him known and to preach the gospel, we must not confuse passion with arrogance. It is from a position of humility that we will most readily be received. Humility is seen in our sensitivity and respect for those we are working with as well as those we are serving. Personally, I want to be zealous, but I also want to be wise. I do not want my efforts to be misinterpreted as arrogance or haughtiness. It is in humility of heart that we can best display the bowl and towel.

It takes humility to do menial tasks, especially when one has authority, education or wealth. If we boast, it can never be because we have attained these things but because His grace has saved and empowered us, granting us the privilege to serve the servants. Very seldom does the superior serve the weaker. Even though Nehemiah was cupbearer to a king, the king asked him what he wanted (Nehemiah 2:4). As a rule, people serve kings rather than being served by them, but this was an example of authority and humility working together. We know that we are to resist the devil and he will flee, but we do not always remember that we must first submit to God (James 4:7); this is another example of authority and humility flowing together. Authority is seen in the humble heart, and humility is not weakness but is actually one of the greatest demonstrations of strength.

> ➤ **They serve with faithfulness.**

To be faithful is to be "steadfast in affection or allegiance, conscientious and firm in adherence to promises or in observance of duty."

Not so with My servant Moses; He is faithful in all My house. (Numbers 12:7)

Then I will raise up for Myself a faithful priest who shall do according to what is in My heart and in My mind. I will build him a sure house, and he shall walk before My anointed forever. (1 Samuel 2:35)

Who then is a faithful and wise servant, whom his master made ruler over his household, to give them food in due season? (Matthew 24:45)

His lord said to him, 'Well done, good and faithful servant; you were faithful over a few things, I will make you ruler over many things. Enter into the joy of your lord.' (Matthew 25:21)

Whoever is faithful in a very little is faithful also in much; and whoever is dishonest in a very little is dishonest also in much. If then you have not been faithful with the dishonest wealth, who will entrust to you the true riches? And if you have not been faithful with what belongs to another, who will give you what is your own? (Luke 16:10-12)

Moreover, it is required of stewards that they be found trustworthy. (1 Corinthians 4:2)

So that you also may know how I am and what I am doing, Tychicus will tell you everything. He is a dear brother and a faithful minister in the Lord. (Ephesians 6:21)

God looks for faithfulness in the servant. He does not require our skills or efforts as much as our faithfulness. Skills are important, but it is faithfulness even in the small things that allows Him to promote us to greater and more prominent roles. All ministry must be carried out by loyal, trustworthy people. It is what God sees and rewards.

> ➤ **They serve in the name of the Lord.**

And whatever you do in word or deed, do all in the name of the Lord Jesus, giving thanks to God the Father through Him. (Colossians 3:17)

Bondservants, be obedient to those who are your masters according to the flesh, with fear and trembling, in sincerity of heart, as to Christ; not with eyeservice, as men-pleasers, but as bondservants of Christ, doing the will of God from the heart, with goodwill doing service, as to the Lord, and not to men, knowing that whatever good anyone does, he will receive the same from the

Lord, whether he is a slave or free. And you, masters, do the same things to them, giving up threatening, knowing that your own Master also is in heaven, and there is no partiality with Him. (Ephesians 6:5-9)

Serving in the name of the Lord is to serve from the position of authority. The name represents power and authority, so even though we serve with humility, at the same time we serve with the authority and the dignity that the name holds. Every knee will bow at that name. Demons flee at that name. We pray for the sick in that name. We wash dirty feet or dirty cars in that name. In other words, we do not go in our own name or title, but in the authority and the majesty of that name. There is no higher name that one can operate in than the name of Jesus.

Winning the World with a Toilet Brush and a Bible

With a toilet brush in one hand and a Bible in the other, we will win our world, grow the Church, and God will get the glory. True greatness is found in serving, not in title or position. At the end of the day, what will count is not what we are known as but what we have done.

Many years ago, we had invited pastors, leaders, and our partners to hear a well-known guest minister speak at our Bible school. As the director of the school, I was elated because everything had come together smoothly and now the place was packed with excited, God-hungry people eagerly awaiting our guest. Then, just moments before I was to introduce him, my maintenance man tapped me on the shoulder and whispered in my ear that all the toilets in the complex had backed up, and we had a mess on our hands (so much for the best-laid plans of mice and men).

In the military, I had dug pit toilets and scrubbed them, but I had never cleaned up backed-up toilets and had never seen such a mess. It would have been easy to ask some of my team to change and help clean up, but the military had taught me never to command a soldier to do something that I would not do myself. With that in mind, I chose to apply this important life lesson: never ask people to do what you would not do or had not done yourself. Handing over the introduction to my wife, I slipped out, changed into work clothes, and began to unstop and clean up the toilet system. At the time it was gross, but now some twenty-five years later I can write about it and affirm that carrying a toilet brush is no different from Jesus carrying the bowl and towel or a few days later serving humanity by carrying the cross.

The Gift of a Toilet Brush

Elhadj Diallo, my dear friend and fellow minister, was serving in his church as an evangelist but was also in charge of keeping the toilets clean. He did both the evangelism and the toilets with a big smile, feeling privileged to be in the work of God. Elhadj lived my saying, "With a toilet brush in one hand and a Bible in the other, we will win our world." At that stage, I did not know him beyond having spotted him while preaching, but I could see the call of God all over his life. I had been teaching a series of meetings called, "The Glory of Serving" (much of this book's content was developed from those teachings).

As a token of our commitment to live as servants of God, I had decided to hand out a few bowls and towels and toilet brushes on the final day of the conference. Packaged in gift wrap and ribbons, I called some people forward to hand these out. Not knowing that Elhadj's job was to clean the toilets, I chose him as one of the recipients of the "gifts." I said something prophetic to him as I handed him the toilet brush, and just a few months later he was called to take over the church as the lead pastor. Elhadj was great in God as a servant and, therefore, God could trust him with the church. He has since planted a number of congregations, his ministry spans several continents, and he is increasing in favor and leadership. To this day he even has the toilet brush hanging on his wall as a symbol of greatness. True greatness is found in the heart of a servant.

In summary:

- As servants, we do not serve for promotion, applause or recognition but because our hearts have become one with His. If the King of the universe came as a servant, then so can we. The motive of our hearts is without any agenda other than to bring pleasure to the heart of God and meet the need of someone else.

- Our heart should desire the mountaintop experience in the glory as well as the desire to meet the needs in the valley below. We need a heart for sitting at the feet of Jesus before casting out demons and touching the untouchable—it is not one or the other but both.

- A true servant will serve with joy, sincerity, love, zeal, humility, and faithfulness and do it all in the name of the Lord.

- With a toilet brush in one hand and a Bible in the other we will win the world! As servants we carry the gospel to the lost, and as servants, we are engaged in all the work of ministry.

Questions:

Is there a difference between the spiritual and the practical? Explain.

What are some wrong motives why people serve?

What are the right motives?

Why does God want us to serve with joy and gladness of heart?

- With sincerity?

- With love?

- With zeal?

- With humility?

- With faithfulness?

Have you been serving with joy? sincerity? love? zeal? humility? faithfulness?

Which area(s) do you need to work on?

Chapter 7

Promotion and Commendation

At that time the disciples came to Jesus, saying, "Who is the greatest in the kingdom of heaven?" (Matthew 18:1)

The disciples always wanted to move to a higher place, just as we do. We want to increase in our ministry, leadership, and authority, moving to a new level and making greater impact. All believers want to succeed in their walk with God and be used by Him. No one who is truly born again wakes up in the morning and says, "Today is a good day not to serve God," or "Today is a good day to live at my lowest level of faith." Every one of us is destined in God to faith, anointing, and service.

These disciples were ambitious. Even at the Last Supper, they were still talking about who among them should be considered the greatest (Luke 22:24). Ambition can either be good or bad; if it is linked to the word "selfish," it is a very dangerous thing indeed.

Let nothing be done through selfish ambition or conceit, but in lowliness of mind let each esteem others better than himself. Let each of you look out not only for his own interests, but also for the interests of others. (Philippians 2:3-4, NKJV)

Ambition is defined as the desire to achieve a particular end or an ardent aspiration for rank, fame or power. Selfish ambition says, "What can I get out of doing this?" and "How will this benefit me?" Whenever self is attached to it, it is a very negative force. In contrast, Kingdom ambition focuses solely on the Lord and desires the advancement of His agenda as an end in itself. If you are ambitious about something but have no motive other than to be of help, that ambition is surely a positive drive. We need people in the Church to have a sense of drive and ambition that is for the will of God to be done.

Faithful servants are recognized and promoted by God.

> ➢ **Joshua was promoted because he was a faithful servant.**

So the LORD spoke to Moses face to face, as a man speaks to his friend. And he would return to the camp, but his servant Joshua the son of Nun, a young man, did not depart from the tabernacle. (Exodus 33:11)

Joshua was called the servant of Moses and was promoted by God because he was a faithful servant. In that verse, the Hebrew word for servant, "sharath," means "to attend as a menial servant or as a worshiper." The word for "worshiper" and the word for "servant" were the same word. Jesus said to the devil, *"For it is written, 'You shall worship the LORD your God, and Him only you shall serve'"* (Luke 4:8). Joshua was a worshiper who loved the presence of God, so when Moses would go back to the camp, Joshua would remain in the glory. He loved God's presence, but worship must be followed by service. Worship will keep your spirit sweet, but service will keep your hands calloused. That is the way of greatness.

> **Elijah separated Elisha to serve.**

While Elisha was plowing with twelve yoke of oxen, Elijah the prophet threw his mantle on him (1 Kings 19:19). After slaughtering his oxen and feeding the people, Elisha *"arose and followed Elijah, and became his servant"* (1 Kings 19:21). Elisha was not known as a prophet but as a servant:

But Jehoshaphat said, 'Is there no prophet of the LORD here, that we may inquire of the LORD by him?' so one of the servants of the king of Israel answered and said, 'Elisha the son of Shaphat is here, who poured water on the hands of Elijah. (2 Kings 3:11)

In the margin of your Bible, you will see that pouring water meant that he was a personal servant of Elijah. Elisha served Elijah for about seventeen years, never prophesying but always just pouring water on his hands and doing what needed to be done. As he did this as an act of his worship and love for God, he served the anointing and served the prophet of God. Seventeen years later, Elijah's mantle fell upon him. The way to increase is to serve. In the same way that Joshua served Moses, Elisha served Elijah, and in so doing served God. Their promotions were directly related to their service to those in leadership above them.

> **Jesus promoted the good and the faithful servants.**

"And he said to him, 'Well done, good servant; because you were faithful in a very little, have authority over ten cities." (Luke 19:17)

In other words, servants who are faithful will be given increase. Promotion comes to the servant-hearted. Though we do not serve to be promoted but out of love, we will find increase in our life when we serve. Promotion and increase come from the Lord. They do not come to the lazy but to the diligent, for the hand of the diligent and faithful will prosper.

Faithfulness is a fruit of the Spirit that should be seen and evidenced in our lives. Jesus was faithful in God's house, being loyal, constant, true to the cause, worthy to be trusted. God does not simply call us to be servants but to be faithful servants. He commends and recognizes good and faithful but rebukes wicked and lazy.

The Way to God's Promotion

Then the mother of Zebedee's sons came to Him with her sons, kneeling down and asking something from Him. (Matthew 20:20)

Now remember that Jesus had already confronted them (Matthew 18:1). He had spoken to them about true greatness, but they wanted to hear it over and over and over. Here again, they are not only ambitious, but their mother is ambitious for them. I wonder if her kneeling was true humility or just ambition manifested in religion.

"And He said to her, 'What do you wish?' She said to Him 'Grant that these two sons of mine may sit, one on Your right hand and the other on the left, in Your kingdom. But Jesus answered and said, 'You do not know what you ask. Are you able to drink the cup that I am about to drink, and be baptized with the baptism that I am baptized with? They said to Him, 'We are able.' So He said to them, 'You will indeed drink My cup, and be baptized with the baptism that I am baptized with; but to sit on My right hand and on My left is not Mine to give, but it is for those for whom it is prepared by My Father.' And when the ten heard it, they were greatly displeased with the two brothers. (Matthew 20:21-24)

No doubt the other disciples were saying to one another, "Jesus taught us what greatness is, and you two brothers are just not listening." What displeased Jesus was not that they did not listen but that they approached greatness from a worldly point of view. It was actually not Jesus but rather the ten who were displeased with James and John. Jesus wanted to bring this subject of greatness into perspective, so He called them all to Himself and gave a little pep talk:

*But Jesus called them to Himself and said, "You know that the rulers of the Gentiles lord it over them, and those who are great exercise authority over them. Yet it shall not be so among you; but **whoever desires** to become great among you, let him be your servant.* (Matthew 20:25-26)

Jesus was not against their aspiration for greatness but against the false, worldly view, which says that greatness is power, authority, and position. He wanted to bring them back to Kingdom principles, demonstrating that His Kingdom is different from the world's kingdom. Greatness in the world's kingdom consists of position and power, but the Kingdom of God does not operate as the world does. He wanted them to realize that Kingdom greatness is found in serving.

*And whoever desires to be first among you, let him be your slave—just as the Son of Man did not come to be served, but to serve, and to **give** His life a ransom for many.* (Matthew 20:27-28)

Will you pay the price?

Jesus says that there is nothing wrong with aspiring to greatness, because greatness in the Kingdom requires you to become a servant. Are you willing to pay the price? The greater your position and authority in the Kingdom of God, the greater your serving role will be. This means that the higher you go in the Kingdom, the greater the load you bear, because you are actually at the bottom holding everything up. The Kingdom of God is really an upside down Kingdom, because up is down and down is up. It is not so much people going upwards, but downwards in this Kingdom.

Do you want to be great? Bear the load, take responsibility for the lives of others, and serve them. **That** is greatness in God's Kingdom. Unfortunately, the modern Church world really does not exemplify that; many in church leadership today look more like CEOs operating in the world system than in the spirit of Christ. As a result, they are unreachable, untouchable, and have no time for the very ones their gift is designed to help—people!

Leadership in Christ's Kingdom is the opposite—it requires the laying down of one's life in greater serving, giving, and sacrificing. Anyone can be great in God's Kingdom, but who will take the responsibility seriously enough to do what is necessary? You should want to be nothing less than what God has called you to be. You should desire to advance in the Kingdom and get as close as possible to the Throne. You should desire to do the works of God, to be mighty in faith, to be strong in anointing. You should desire intensity in your passion and your love for God. If you want to be great, take the way of the cross, of the bowl and towel.

We hear about taking the cross, but not about taking the bowl and towel and becoming a servant, and **then** sacrificing our life and our time. Jesus **gave** His life, so now we give **our** lives, **our** time, and **our** energy, not for salvation, but because we so highly value His sacrifice. If you want to be great, then give, serve, and lay down your life.

Jesus gave His life as a servant not only at the Cross, but throughout His ministry as He carried the burdens of the weak, feeding them and meeting them in their suffering. He was a servant who became the suffering servant at Calvary, serving humanity by willingly taking upon Himself the punishment that we deserve.

Servants are selfless.

Just as Jesus gave Himself to serve us, servants will give of themselves. Translate your desire for greatness into servanthood by becoming one who will give your life. There is nothing wrong with aiming for greatness in God, because He is a great God and wants you to achieve great things.

William Carey (1761-1834), the English missionary who is called "the father of modern missions," said, "Attempt great things for God." It is good to attempt great things for God and to believe Him to do a work through your life. Some are satisfied with one soul and others with ten, but I am believing for cities and nations, not in order to be seen but simply to serve.

If we have no interest in attempting great things for God such as winning souls or touching lives, we are backslidden and need help. Having no desire for increase in God or for greater anointing and greater results indicates that we are carnal and operating as mere men. When the disciples said to Jesus, "Increase our faith," He did not rebuke them. He never rebuked those who wanted to walk and work in the supernatural but rather commended them. He only cautioned, "Make sure that your values and your motives are right."

It is not about trying to build a name for yourself, but going to the place where you take on more responsibility. Promotion in the Kingdom of God means that you are given a greater entrustment, and with this greater entrustment comes greater responsibility. So every time that you say, "More, Lord," you are actually saying, "Make me accountable to a greater degree."

Isaiah speaks about the suffering servant: *"Behold, My Servant shall deal prudently; He shall be exalted and extolled and be very high....Surely He has borne our griefs and carried our sorrows"* (Isaiah 52:13, 53:4). A servant bears the load. Jesus was the suffering servant who not only taught and ministered from a servant heart by doing what needed to be done, but who also demonstrated it at the Cross.

As a result of His faithful serving, God highly exalted Him. He gave Jesus the position of King of kings and Lord of lords, granting Him all authority in heaven and earth. In the same way, we who are faithful as servant-hearted followers of Jesus will be promoted in due time.

Humble yourselves in the sight of the Lord, and He will lift you up. (James 4:10)

As we serve Jesus in an attitude of humility as servants, He sees our heart and our ways and in due season will promote us. We are not pursuing leadership but rather the privilege to serve; then as we do this, there will come a time when God will give us authority, leadership, and power.

Promotion comes from the Lord; His eyes are going to and fro in search of loyal sons and daughters, faithful servants, and humble hearts. As He finds these, He gives them increase as well as the ability to handle what He confers. We need to be patient because the process of God's promotion takes time. To understand that there are no overnight successes in the Kingdom, we need look no further than the biblical account of Joseph. After years of faithful service in Potiphar's house, a false accusation landed him in prison. It might seem that Joseph went from prison to the right hand of Pharaoh in a day, but his promotion actually took thirteen long, arduous years. Just seventeen years old when he had the dream, it was not until he was thirty years old that he stood before Pharaoh as the second most powerful man in Egypt (Genesis 37:2-5; 41:46). There must have been many days, months, and years when Joseph wondered if his dream of being a leader would ever become a reality. In all that time he was being developed in character to handle authority. If we cannot serve, we cannot rule.

For exaltation comes neither from the east nor from the west nor from the south. But God is the Judge: He puts down one, And exalts another. (Psalms 75:6-7)

Having been faithful to invest the talents he was entrusted with, the servant heard these words, *"Well done, good and faithful servant; you were faithful over a few things, I will make you ruler over many things"* (Matthew 25:21).

Nehemiah had been faithful as cupbearer to the king, and when he stood in the gap interceding for the destroyed city of Jerusalem, God promoted this servant to become a great leader.

Author and preacher Charles Swindoll put it succinctly, "In God's family, there is to be one great body of people: servants." In fact, that is the way to the top in His Kingdom. The way up is the way down. The way to grow and the way to promotion in God is to be a servant. We are citizens of that Kingdom. We are the family of God, and God's family is like Jesus, servants in attitude.

In summary:

- Jesus is not opposed to His servants desiring to be great, as long as this greatness is acquired in the right way. True greatness is bearing the load and responsibility for others; it means being willing to serve and sacrifice. Do we have any candidates?

- Selfish ambition is dangerous, but godly ambition to do great works for the Lord is to be encouraged.

- All servants who are faithful are candidates for promotion.

- The doors of opportunity stand wide open for anyone to be great in the Kingdom, but in order to qualify, one must become the least by becoming a servant and sacrificing. This leaves no room for an ego!

Questions:

What is greatness according to the world?

What is greatness according to God?

Is it wrong to desire to be great in the Kingdom? Explain.

Can anyone be great in God's Kingdom? Explain.

Are you a candidate for greatness in God's Kingdom?

Are you willing to serve and sacrifice?

Explain the two kinds of ambition.

Would you say that you are ambitious? In what way?

Could this lead to competiveness with other Christians?

Well Done...good and faithful servant

Why do you think that the path to increase is the way of the servant?

Joshua, Elisha, Nehemiah, and Joseph were all promoted. Why?

Chapter 8

Becoming More Like Jesus

For even the Son of Man did not come to be served, but to serve, and to give His life a ransom for many. (Mark 10:45)

Jesus Christ did not come to be served but to serve. He stripped Himself and took up the bowl and towel to wash the disciples' feet, but He went way beyond that teaching moment. He served humanity by going to the Cross and laying down His very life. His extraordinary act of selfless love secured a way for the whole world to know God and live free from the punishment and burden of our sins. This act of redemption was the purest form of servanthood. Jesus said, *"As the Father has sent Me, I also send you"* (John 20:21); therefore, anyone desiring to make a difference to this generation will need to become like Jesus and become a servant. How did Jesus operate in His ministry on earth?

- He was anointed.
- He was motivated by genuine love.
- He was a servant.
- He laid down His life.

I suggest that we arise to the call of God and operate in the same way as Jesus, having the attitude of a servant

(Philippians 2:5-7). If we truly want to become more like Jesus, we must become servants.

- We must be anointed.
- We must be motivated by genuine love.
- We must be servants.
- We must lay down our lives.

The Love of God in Action

Many years ago in the early days of my ministry, we had experienced severe flooding in certain areas of South Africa. Numerous homes were destroyed and entire communities were left stranded. My wife and I were able to raise money, food, water, clothing, and blankets, and with the support of the South African Defense Force, I was able to transport these provisions. Together with the supplies, I sent about thirty of my staff and students to go and help clean the houses of mud and debris. Staying for two months to work in the area, hearts were won to the Lord as a result of my team ministering the love of God and the gospel of Christ while working with them.

Unfortunately, we discovered that there were churches just outside the flood zone that did absolutely nothing to help these people. Since we had traveled hundreds of miles to get there to assist them, many of these new believers asked us why we had come from such a distance, yet their own churches would not travel down the road to help them. I explained that this was the love of God being demonstrated in compassion, kindness, and with serving hands. I also had to explain that not all who profess to be followers of God will serve and sacrifice. The difference was that we acted upon the Word, but those churches did not. True faith is not found in intentions and promises but in action.

Regrettably, many professing followers of Jesus all over the world will not go a few miles down the road to serve or help someone else. They remind us of the priest and the Levite who passed by on the other side of the street to avoid having to deal with the poor soul who had been beaten and robbed and left for dead.

Then Jesus answered and said: "A certain man went down from Jerusalem to Jericho, and fell among thieves, who stripped him of his clothing, wounded him, and departed, leaving him half dead. Now by chance a certain priest came down that road. And when he saw him, he passed by on the other side. Likewise a Levite, when he arrived at the place, came and looked, and passed by on the other side. But a certain Samaritan, as he journeyed, came where he was. And when he saw him, he had compassion. So he went to him and bandaged his wounds, pouring on oil and wine; and he set him on his own animal, brought him to an inn, and took care of him. On the next day, when he departed, he took out two denarii, gave them to the innkeeper, and said to him, 'Take care of him; and whatever more you spend, when I come again, I will repay you.' So which of these three do you think was neighbor to him who fell among the thieves?" And he said, "He who showed mercy on him." Then Jesus said to him, "Go and do likewise." (Luke 10:30-37)

Happily, there are those compelled by the love of God who will travel long distances to serve and aid someone in distress and need. This book is an appeal to become one of them.

Sacrifices must be made in order to serve.

We need to have the same attitude as Jesus. To what point? Even to the point of death, to the place where we lose what is rightfully ours. Willingly we lay it all down for someone else and for the glory of His name. This sense of selflessness and sacrifice is captured in the various hymns and worship songs that deal with surrender. We gladly sing these songs about laying down our rights and counting everything loss for the sake of bringing Him glory, but are we singing from our hearts or our lips? I have a saying, "Easier sung than done." So many people have sung these songs yet hold on to their rights, their time, their money, and their entrusted God-given abilities. Surrender is the language of the servant. We are not scared away from our destiny because of loss or suffering because it is the way of the Master—the way of the bowl and towel and the way of the cross. This is the path to doing a great work to the glory of God.

We all know John 3:16—"For God so loved the world...." But can we so readily quote 1 John 3:16? It says, *"By this we know love, because He laid down His life for us. And we also ought to lay down our lives for the brethren."*

You lay down your life for someone else by laying down your rights, what you feel, what you think, what is rightfully yours. Love always surrenders and love always sacrifices, even to the point of laying down one's life. This was evidenced in Jesus and then in His passionate followers.

Paul also made himself a servant: *"For though I am free from all men, I have made myself a servant to all"* (1 Corinthians 9:19). His freedom drove him to willingly become a servant, not to do his own thing and have his own way, but to help others. He did this in his attitude. By serving the people God had sent him to reach, he was able to win them: *"For though I am free from all men, I have made myself a servant to all, that I might win the more"* (1 Corinthians 9:19). We serve people to win them, but if they are already "won," we can still serve them by winning them to a deeper walk with God and to the place of God's provision. When you serve, you are always winning someone. Having the heart of a servant will always cause you to win and be victorious in your life.

*For you, brethren, have been called to liberty; only do not use liberty as an opportunity for the flesh, but **through love serve one another.**"* (Galatians 5:13)

That is the attitude of Jesus, the motive of Jesus, the heart of God. Love is the motive that causes us in our freedom to serve one another.

Describing the Person and the Ministry of a Servant

The ministry of a servant is best expressed in the spirit of humility. Jesus, our model, humbled Himself and made Himself of no reputation. This is not weakness but actually the true test of character. We are secure in our identity as sons and daughters of God but servants to humanity and the Church.

Being a servant is practical yet is always spiritual. Serving is not considered a burden or a chore; it demands no thanks or acknowledgment, because it is done to the Lord spontaneously and generously. We should not wait for an invitation to serve but freely choose to do it.

Being a servant is laying down your life and being selfless. The dearth of evangelism has usually been blamed on apathy and indifference, but the real culprit is selfishness. People cannot serve God if they are selfish and self-centered, but once they become Christ-centered, they will make an impact. My prayer is that we will see many people raised up with a passion like Mother Teresa's. She gained world prominence as the most important woman of the 20th century. She did not have great oratorical or leadership skills, but she did have something that should be found in every servant: the willingness to have compassion on the suffering of the world and to translate that into action.

Compassion made her great. Her brokenness and selflessness took her to the gutters of Calcutta to work among the sick and the dying and to touch them. Servants feel the suffering of others. She never looked for fame, yet when she died she was the most famous woman of her century. She never even needed to carry a passport, because her face was her passport wherever she went—the world knew her. As a world ambassador for peace and healing because of a serving heart, her fame enabled her to address kings and world leaders on the issues of compassion. She never served to gain prominence or support for her ventures but simply because no one else was doing it. God then used her compassionate heart and raised her up. She was not looking for promotion or fame but only wanted to meet a need, and that is what servants do. Servants are moved by compassion and do **what** is needed to be done **when** it is needed to be done. Selflessness takes us beyond our own world into prayer, giving, serving, out of our world into His.

The Power of Serving

Being a servant is very powerful. The symbol of serving—the bowl and towel—is a symbol of power.

The symbol of the cross is a symbol of redemption and is also powerful. The symbol of the Holy Spirit is the dove, and His work certainly is very powerful. Nevertheless, the power is not actually in the symbol but rather in what each of these images represents. The cross, the dove, and the bowl and towel are all symbols of unusual yet powerful work being accomplished.

Serving can bring the focus of Jesus to your life and to your ministry. Woodrow Wilson said, "The princes among us are those who forget themselves and serve mankind." True greatness is found in humbling yourself and serving others. Even if people do not acknowledge what you do as being powerful, do not be concerned; you can be sure that God will reward and promote those who humbly serve.

The selfishness that is rampant in the Body of Christ today must be replaced by selflessness and a life dedicated to the cause of the Kingdom. God is calling us to a higher level of servanthood where we will serve Him, our families, our church, and the nations of the world.

We need to turn things around. We can look at what is wrong in the church and blame those who are passive, or we can begin to stir people back to their first love where God's priorities are restored to their rightful place. Until every child of God becomes a dedicated member of the ministry team of the Body of Christ, our potential to reveal the glory of God to our generation will remain dormant. It is time for spectators to break out of their comfort zones and join the team. The outcome will depend on our full participation. Reaching our generation with the gospel will require nothing less than every Christian taking his or her place in devoted service. Will you report for duty today?

Everyone knows that problems abound in the Body of Christ. We have corruption, immorality, failed marriages, to name but a few, and, thus, it would appear that we live our lives no differently from the world. Jesus warned us that a little leaven (of sin or compromise) affects the whole batch, but this can have positive implications if we speak of the leaven of righteousness and revival; these can also spread and beneficially affect the whole batch.

We need a revival not only of miracles and salvations, but also of mobilization that will provoke and propel **everyone** into the work of ministry. Such a revival will awaken the onlookers out of their slumber of apathy, complacency, and inertia. Can you imagine the extraordinary momentum that will be gained in evangelism, prayer, discipleship, and compassionate caring as every Christian rises to the call of God?

Become part of the solution, not a continued part of the problem. Living in neutrality by doing nothing is just as bad as doing evil because each does damage to the Church. Passivity keeps the Church from moving forward. When all believers get busy serving God according to their giftings and callings, we will begin to take ground and see nations rocked by the gospel.

Another saying of mine is, "Every member a minister" (servant). Just think what would happen if every Christian became a minister and began to participate in the responsibility of the gospel and the work of growing the Church. In the days of Nehemiah, when the destroyed city of Jerusalem was being rebuilt, everyone had a mind to work. Despite an extremely hostile environment, there were no spectators or casual bystanders, but **all** threw themselves fully into the task of rebuilding. As a result of the grace of God and the synergistic power of this combined effort, the walls were rebuilt in just fifty-two days. Notice that the leaders and the people joined forces under the leadership of Nehemiah and began to work:

Then I said to them, "You see the distress that we are in, how Jerusalem lies waste, and its gates are burned with fire. Come and let us build the wall of Jerusalem, that we may no longer be a reproach." And I told them of the hand of my God which had been good upon me, and also of the king's words that he had spoken to me. So they said, "Let us rise up and build." ***Then they set their hands to this good work.*** *(Nehemiah 2:17-18)*

In the face of open hostility, the walls were being rebuilt because the people—not just some but all—cooperated in the work. Do you see that when everyone was busy, the work advanced by leaps and bounds?

*So we built the wall, and the entire wall was joined together up to half its height, **for the people had a mind to work**.* (Nehemiah 4:6)

In the Hebrew, having "a mind" to work means that they had a heart to work, i.e., their heart was in it. This was not a superficial or token effort, but they labored with great energy and zeal.

Realizing that the joint efforts of the people would get the job done, the harassment by their enemies intensified when the wall was at half its height. Some probably stopped working because this harassment had begun to affect their morale, but Nehemiah's strong leadership managed to get every single one of them to return to the task at hand. As a result, the people stayed the course and all went back to work.

*And it happened, when our enemies heard that it was known to us, and that God had brought their plot to nothing, that **all of us** returned to the wall, everyone to his work.* (Nehemiah 4:15)

In just fifty-two days the people did the impossible, through God's grace and their combined efforts.

*So the wall was finished on the twenty-fifth day of Elul, in fifty-two days. And it happened, when all our enemies heard of it, and all the nations around us saw these things, that they were very disheartened in their own eyes; for they perceived **that this work was done by our God**.* (Nehemiah 6:15-16)

I believe that **if** every member of the Body of Christ became a minister and we united in our strategy for world harvest and building the Church, we would accomplish the impossible. The God who caused the city of Nineveh to be changed in just one day will help us. The God who caused the people to join forces to rebuild Jerusalem in just fifty-two days will be on our side. Through our God, we shall do valiantly. We shall do great exploits and see miraculous progress.

Servants do not wait to be asked to serve but are quick to take initiative and do what needs to be done spontaneously. I urge you not to wait but to dive in. Begin to live as a servant of the Lord, because this is the unstoppable love of God operating in your life, compelling you to make a difference to this generation. I believe that we can start a movement of servanthood that will become viral in a positive way. May every servant be infectious with passion, spreading this holy love in action until everyone rises to become part of the ministry team. Let us commit to begin today...right now! Open your heart to the Holy Spirit and ask Him to touch and empower you to serve, and then go for it!

Get involved.

It is said that the way to hell is paved with good intentions. Many in the Body of Christ want to do something great for God one day. They have good intentions, and they certainly mean well, but without actually getting involved, their great potential will remain untapped and unfulfilled. You must not mark time until circumstances come together perfectly, because they rarely will. You just have to seize the day. If the farmer waited for the perfect conditions, he might never get his crops sown or his fields harvested.

He who observes the wind will not sow, and he who regards the clouds will not reap. (Ecclesiastes 11:4)

There is no time like the present; today is the best day to start being active in ministry. You can start by calling your church office and asking where help is needed. It is almost a certainty that you will be told that the nursery could use your help. Even in healthy churches that have an abundance of volunteers, the nursery is nearly always understaffed. If you have graphics, web, or secretarial skills, you can offer to assist your church or a Christian ministry for a few hours a week, thus saving them thousands of dollars a year. If the church has no areas for involvement, you are probably in glory and just have not realized it yet! Or maybe your reputation precedes you, and your help is not wanted because you are a problem waiting to happen. In this case, you may need to get in a ministry line for a huge overhaul. If there is genuinely no area open for involvement, find a needy ministry or charitable organization and volunteer your services. Visit a widow and take her out for a meal (or better still, make her a meal) or drive an elderly neighbor to an appointment or to do some shopping. What about washing someone's car, which is surely less embarrassing than washing feet? The point is to find something to do and then serve in a caring way.

Areas in the church where you can begin serving:

- Nursery
- Cleaning
- Maintenance
- Parking
- Greeting
- Ushering
- Sound
- Administration
- Hospitality
- Intercession

Areas outside the church:

- Assist a missionary organization with administration.
- Get involved in Habitat for Humanity, Meals on Wheels, or Big Brothers Big Sisters.
- Help out in a soup kitchen or food bank.

- Volunteer at a hospital to greet visitors or visit patients.

- Spend time with residents in a nursing home.

- Teach English to an immigrant.

Your act of service may not bring you a financial return, but it will be something that God will see and reward. When all is said and done, the words that you will hear are, "Well done, good and faithful servant!"

In summary:

- Do not be like those who live down the road from people in dire straits and do nothing about it (or even worse, like those who watch as someone else travels from afar because you refuse to be involved). This is what the priest and the Levite did in the account of the Good Samaritan. They left the task of care and compassion to someone else.

- One of the reasons many avoid serving and prefer to be served is that being a servant will require sacrifice. It is easier to have someone serve you than to be the one serving, because it will cost you time and effort. As a servant you will have to go out of your way.

- The qualities found in a servant are humility, selflessness, compassion, and faithfulness.

Well Done...good and faithful servant

- True greatness is found in being a servant.

Questions:

In Nehemiah's time, the wall that had been destroyed in Jerusalem was rebuilt in only 52 days. What made this possible?

Doing nothing is just as damaging to the Church as doing evil. Explain.

We have all sung songs in church about surrendering all. Can you say that you have surrendered all? Explain.

The qualities of a servant are humility, selflessness, compassion, and faithfulness. Do you have each of these qualities?

What do you think it will take to get Christians to serve?

How has your concept of serving changed since you began this Bible study?

Will you begin the servant lifestyle today?